KATHLEEN T.
HORNING

FROM COVER TO COVER

Evaluating
and Reviewing
Children's Books

REVISED EDITION

Collins
An Imprint of HarperCollinsPublishers

Collins is an imprint of HarperCollins Publishers.
From Cover to Cover: Evaluating and Reviewing Children's Books
(Revised Edition)
Copyright © 1997, 2010 by Kathleen T. Horning

Library of Congress Cataloging-in-Publication Data
Horning, Kathleen T.
        From cover to cover : evaluating and reviewing children's books / Kathleen T.
Horning. — Rev. ed.
        p. cm.
        Includes bibliographical references and index.
        ISBN 978-0-06-077756-2 (trade bdg.)
        ISBN 978-0-06-077757-9 (pbk. bdg.)
        1. Book reviewing.   2. Children's literature—History and criticism.
3. Children—Books and reading.   I. Title.
PN98.B7H67   2010   2009027564
028.1'62—dc22   CIP
                                                                          AC

Typography by Andrea Vandergrift
10 11 12 13 14   LP/RRDH   10 9 8 7 6 5 4 3 2 1
❖
Revised edition, 2010

FROM COVER TO COVER

Evaluating
and Reviewing
Children's Books

REVISED EDITION

For Emily

ACKNOWLEDGMENTS

The idea for this book was first suggested to me by my friend Ruth Gordon, librarian, writer, anthologist, and an extraordinary critic in her own right. I would like to thank her for suggesting it and for trusting me to do it. I would also like to acknowledge Robert O. Warren, who edited the first edition of *From Cover to Cover*, and Phoebe Yeh, who edited this current edition. Their unflagging enthusiasm for the book has been an inspiration.

The work could not have been completed without the fine children's literature collection at the Cooperative Children's Book Center, a library of the School of Education, University of Wisconsin–Madison. My colleagues at the Cooperative Children's Book Center have enthusiastically offered their support and encouragement. I am indebted to director emerita, Ginny Moore Kruse, my friend and mentor, who has guided my professional growth from the first day I entered the CCBC; and to my fellow CCBC librarians, Merri Lindgren, Tessa Michaelson, Hollis Rudiger, and Megan Schliesman, who have greatly enriched the workplace with their intellect, insight, and good humor and who make it a pleasure to come to work every day. Regular participants in the CCBC's monthly book discussions have generously shared their time and their opinions about new children's books and have helped hone my critical skills. My friends and colleagues in other fields, who share their perspectives and wisdom, continually broaden my understanding of children's books. I would especially like to acknowledge and thank first-grade teacher Margaret Jensen, who has helped me understand how children learn to read and how to evaluate books that make it possible for them to do so. Lastly I would like to acknowledge my partner, Emily Kokie, for her encouragement and support.

CONTENTS

INTRODUCTION

With approximately five thousand new books for children being published every year, it may seem an overwhelming task to wade through them. But with this embarrassment of riches, it is important for adults who work with children and books to sharpen their critical skills so they can select the best books available. But how do we determine which books are the best ones? What makes a good children's book? Are there simple standards we can apply across the board? Or are there different sets of standards for different types of books? Or for different needs or audiences? This book is meant to serve as a beginning place for those who want to evaluate or review books published specifically for children. It will provide concrete examples of aspects to consider when looking at children's books with a critical eye.

DISTINCTIONS BETWEEN EVALUATION AND REVIEW

For our purposes, we will use the term *evaluation* to refer to a critical assessment of a book—in other words, the thought process one goes through in order to formulate an opinion of the book. Sometimes book evaluation can be done very quickly, drawing on a wealth of professional or personal experience; other times it requires a great deal of deliberation, careful thinking, perhaps even consultation with outside sources of information. This book will offer guidelines for evaluating the various genres of children's books: nonfiction, folklore, poetry, picture books, beginning readers and easy chapter books, and fiction. It will also offer advice on how to write a review.

A *review* is a formal written expression of the critical assessment, generally printed soon after the book under consideration has been published. Good reviews help readers create a mental picture of the book by briefly describing it and presenting an assessment of its quality.

WHAT MAKES A GOOD CHILDREN'S BOOK?
There are no quick, easy answers to this question because there are so many different kinds of children's books that can be outstanding for different reasons. Furthermore, as times change and our perception of children evolves, so too do our standards for excellence in children's books. Each chapter in this book will open with a brief history that will help provide a context for the type of books under discussion, followed by evaluative criteria, using examples from outstanding books. Newcomers to the field may wish to seek out these exemplary books to expand their general knowledge of children's literature by reading some of the best books we offer children.

NEW TO THE SECOND EDITION
It's been more than ten years since the first edition of *From Cover to Cover* was published, and in that time there have been changes in the

children's book world. The chapters included here have been updated to reflect that, and the chapter on fiction now includes a section on subgenres. In each chapter new books have been included as examples of some of the best that children's literature has to offer.

CHAPTER 1

A Critical Approach to Children's Books

Reading a book for the purposes of evaluation and review requires more attention to detail than reading a book for pleasure or for information. When you read to evaluate, your assessment of the book will ultimately affect other potential readers. It may make a difference as to whether or not a book is purchased for a library or a school or as a birthday gift for a child you'll never meet. In fact, it may make a difference as to whether or not the book is read by a child at all. It is your professional responsibility to try to take your evaluation beyond a personal response.

This is not to say that your personal response doesn't matter. It would be impossible for you to put it completely aside—you are a reviewer, after all, not a robot. What the responsible reviewer strives for is an informed and reasoned opinion, clearly articulated so that others can learn about books they haven't read.

In essence, a children's book reviewer reads and writes with two audiences in mind: (1) adults who read reviews to help them select books for children and (2) the children themselves. If a review is printed in a publication that has a national distribution, it may also be read by the author and publisher of the book in question; however, neither is the intended audience for your review. In other words, it is not your goal to write a review to stroke an author's ego or to pick a bone with a publisher.

Still, it is important to remember that most books for children are created with the best intentions in mind. No one sets out to produce a crummy book that kids will hate. If this is your initial assessment of a book you're reviewing, it would be unfair and unwise to let it stand as your final one without a great deal of further consideration. You'll need to take a closer look at the book. What was the author's intent in writing the book? What qualities did the editor see that led him or her to believe that the book merited publication? Why did the illustrator choose this particular style? The answers to all these questions have their origins in the history of the book's creation. While it isn't necessary for you to know the details of a book's publishing history in order to review it, an understanding of the general context in which children's books are created will help you read more critically.

HOW CHILDREN'S BOOKS ARE PUBLISHED

Many publishing houses have divisions or departments that are devoted to publishing books for young people. These were, for the most part, established in the 1920s and developed through the pioneering efforts of women such as Louise Seaman Bechtel, May Massee, Helen Dean Fish, Marian Fiery, and Virginia Kirkus, who were the first children's book editors. Unlike adult book divisions, which are driven by the consumer market (bookstore sales), children's book divisions developed largely in response to an institutional market. Sales to libraries and schools accounted for a high percentage of the total number of children's books sold. As library budgets began to shrink in the 1970s and 1980s, children's book publishers began to turn their attention toward consumer sales as well, although the institutional market continues to be an important influence in the children's book industry.

There are books that are created specifically for one market or the other. Those that are produced for the institutional school market alone are called *textbooks*. They are generally sold to entire school districts rather than to individuals. They are also created in a separate division of the publishing industry that specializes in producing books to fit the exact needs of teachers working with specific school curricula and guidelines at various grade levels. Books that are produced with only the consumer market in mind are called *mass-market books*. These are generally produced as paperbacks or as picture books with inexpensive cardboard covers (such as Little Golden Books) and they may be sold in supermarkets, airports, drugstores, and convenience stores as well as in bookstores. While there are publishers that specialize in producing mass-market books, most children's book departments produce mass-market books to some degree.

Books created for both the consumer market and the institutional market are called *trade books*. These are sold to schools and libraries, and they are also sold directly to consumers through bookstores. Both quality and child appeal are taken into account when weighing the sales potential. From the publisher's point of view, the best kind of children's trade book is one that will succeed in both the consumer and the institutional market and will continue to sell well for decades. This is the type of success guaranteed by a book that wins the Newbery or Caldecott Medal.

Most children's books start out as an idea in the mind of an author. That may seem obvious to you, but I mention it here because many people seem to have the notion that ideas start with publishers, who then assign them to authors. People often ask children's editors: "Why don't you publish more books about X?" in a tone that suggests they hold editors personally responsible for the lack of X books. But editors don't tell authors what to write. They must wait for X to develop in the mind of the author, and then they have to determine if it's good enough to publish. The editor's role is to find and nurture the talents of authors and artists who will create good children's books. If they cast their nets widely enough, their catch may include an author who will come up with the idea of writing about X on his or her own.

Once a manuscript is accepted for publication, the editor works with the author to help shape the book into its final form. An editor may make suggestions about chapters that need to be rewritten, characters that need to be developed, or ideas that need to be clarified. The ultimate responsibility for the writing, however, rests with the author. If the author has submitted the text for a picture book, the editor will choose an artist to illustrate it. While the author may see preliminary sketches of the illustrations, chances are that the author and illustrator will never meet while the book is in production. Generally the author has very little to say about the illustrations other than their factual content.

When the final version of the manuscript is completed, the editor—in conjunction with the designers—will estimate the number of pages there will be in the printed book, specify the *trim* (size of page), and decide the type of binding. He or she will also discuss jacket art with the art director, who will in turn assign the work to an artist if it's not an illustrated book; most picture book jackets are illustrated by the artist doing the interior art. Again, the author generally has little or no say in such matters. The manuscript is turned over to a *copy editor*, who will read it to correct spelling, grammar, and inconsistencies in style and internal plot. A copy editor may question noticeable errors in fact but will not retrace every step of an author's background research. In most cases the author has final say about the copy editor's changes.

A copy of the manuscript is also given to a *designer*, who will choose an appropriate *typeface*. Based on the number of *characters* (letters, numbers, spaces, and punctuation marks) in the final manuscript, the designer will choose a typeface that will fill the number of pages estimated earlier.

The designer may print out sample pages at this point so that the editor can look at the *page layout* (what the printed page in the book will look like) and decide if the type and page design are appropriate for the look of the book. The size of type in a children's book is especially important, as it often dictates the age level of the book's audience. Children are surprisingly sensitive to typeface. If they decide it's too small, they're likely to reject a book as "too hard," no matter the content. If they decide it's too large, they may scoff at a book as "babyish."

When the editor and designer have made the final decisions about typeface, number of lines per page, margins, and other design elements, the manuscript is set into pages. Computer-generated page proofs are circulated for proofreading and final corrections. An author rarely makes any substantive changes in the text at this point, although the author, editor, designer, and a proofreader will look at the proofs carefully in case there are any printer's errors or any blatant mistakes that were somehow missed earlier. Meanwhile, the sales department estimates the number of copies in the initial print run. The production department will arrange to have paper—chosen for its color, weight, and cost—and material for the binding, often chosen to coordinate with the jacket, sent to the printer. The final approved pages are sent to the printer for the actual edition run.

Because of the visual nature of picture books, they undergo a different production process. After an artist has been commissioned to illustrate a picture book, he or she discusses layout and design with the editor and the art director and makes preliminary decisions about how each page will look. Next he or she prepares and submits *roughs*, detailed pencil sketches for each page spread. Usually, the designer creates paged layouts placing text with relation to the artist's roughs and the trim size of the book. There can be several layouts or dummy stages before the roughs are approved, and the artist completes and delivers the finished artwork for the book. The designer prepares a camera-ready digital *mechanical* that shows the position of text and illustrations and includes instructions for the printer. The first set of color proofs comes back from the printer, and they are carefully checked against the originals by the artist, art director, designer, and editor so that any problems with color, size, and position of the illustrations can be corrected. When these final decisions and adjustments are made, and after a few more proof stages for final checking, the book goes off to be printed and bound.

In the meantime, the editor has enthusiastically described the book to the company's in-house sales representatives at the seasonal sales conference and has provided a description of the book for them to use in their catalog. They in turn will try to get the book into bookstores across the country. The publisher's marketing and publicity departments have been working on behalf of the book, as well, to get the word out to the world that the book exists. A glowing description of the book will be placed into their print and/or online seasonal catalog. They may include the title in announcement ads of the season's forthcoming books that appear in trade journals such as *Publishers Weekly* and *School Library Journal*. They may choose to buy advertising space in a children's literature review journal that will specifically highlight the book. Or they may create posters, bookmarks, flyers, or buttons advertising the book to give away to librarians and teachers at professional conferences. They may promote the book through their company website, online catalogs, and blogs.

They will also send out *advance review copies* of the book (often specially printed from uncorrected proofs so reviewers can evaluate the book early) to professional journals and to some general publications. In addition, review copies are sent to large library systems and departments of education for their own internal review. Favorable reviews and recommendations for purchase by these large systems can be important to the success of any children's book, since institutional sales still account for a significant part of the children's trade book market. Throughout most of the twentieth century, children's librarians set the critical standards for children's trade books, and they continue to have a great deal of influence in the twenty-first century. The ultimate prizes for a children's author and illustrator are the Newbery and Caldecott Medals, respectively. These are the only book awards that have nationwide impact on sales, and they are given annually by children's librarians under the auspices of the American Library Association.

THE PARTS OF A BOOK

Just as a bit of background about the publishing industry can help to inform your reading, so too can an understanding of the book itself as an object.

For the most part, children's books are still considered as physical entities, although we are at a point in history where technology is rapidly changing. After a few decades of fits and starts, *electronic books*, or *e-books*, have finally become accepted in the adult trade publishing world, but they have been slower to take hold in children's book publishing. While some experts have observed that children, with their affinity for computers and technology, would seem to be a natural audience for e-books, others have pointed out the special challenges the industry faces when it comes to children, from creating a satisfying electronic picture book to issues of access since many children do not own the necessary technical devices needed to read an e-book.

Although books may vary widely, there are several constants in the way they are designed that should be familiar to you. It's useful to know the special vocabulary of the book—to know what endpapers are, for example, or what is meant when someone refers to flap copy. As a critical reader, you should be aware of all the parts of a book that contribute to the whole. You may even find a piece of information in the author's acknowledgments or on the copyright page that will help you with an assessment of the book.

Beyond the body of the book proper, created by an author and/or illustrator, we can look at three additional parts: *binding, front matter,* and *back matter.*

BINDING

The cover: Children are notorious for judging books by their covers and that, of course, is the opposite of what the critic strives for. Most hardcover children's trade books come with a paper jacket, or *dust jacket,* that includes color artwork designed to entice potential readers. The part of the jacket that folds around the inside of the cover is called a *flap,* and it contains printed information, known as *flap copy.* The front flap generally gives a brief summary of the book and typically concludes with a lot of superlatives about how great the book is, while the back flap often includes biographical information (*bio*) about the book's creator(s).

Professional reviewers don't always see the complete dust jacket, as they often see books before they are published, in a form known as *bound galleys* or *advance reading copies* (*ARCs*). Whether you see the jacket or not when you are evaluating a book, it is important to keep in mind that jackets function more as part of a book's marketing and promotion than as an integral part of its art.

Most children's trade books make their first appearance as *hardcover,* or *clothbound,* books. The hard covers, called boards, are composed of heavy cardboard stock covered with cloth or paper, or a combination of the two. *Library bindings* on hardcover books are reinforced to stand up to multiple circulations, whereas *trade bindings* are on books produced primarily for bookstore sales. If a hardcover book sells reasonably well, the publisher may choose to issue a *paperback* edition or may sell the paperback rights to another publisher. In some cases, a publisher opts for *simultaneous publication*, issuing a hardcover and paperback at the same time. Other times, a hardcover edition will be skipped and the book will be issued as a *paperback original*. In young-adult literature, paperback originals have become increasingly common, but in children's books, most paperback originals are published as mass-market books, which are generally not given the same consideration by reviewers. As a result, they are often only briefly noted or even completely overlooked, although they are regularly purchased by libraries due to their popularity. Most popular series books such as Cirque du Freak, Magic Tree House, and Rainbow Magic are issued as paperback originals and thus have rarely withstood the scrutiny of professional evaluation and review because they are not reviewed as individual volumes.

Endpapers: Every hardcover book has sheets of paper, generally of heavier stock than the text, pasted flat against the insides of the front and back covers and along the gutters (the page edges at the inside margins) of the first and last pages of the book. Sometimes endpapers include supplementary information such as maps, and sometimes— particularly in picture books—they are illustrated or the story actually begins and ends on the endpapers. More often than not, endpapers are left blank, although they may be of a color contrasting with or complementary to the cover or the jacket, to add to the overall aesthetic of the book. Books are composed of sheets of paper called leaves. The right-hand page of the leaf is the *recto* page; the page on the reverse side is the *verso* (the left-hand page).

FRONT MATTER

Half title: The first page of a book, bearing only the book's title, with no author or publisher listed. Half-title pages are carryovers from the past, when books were sold without bindings, and half titles served to both identify and protect the pages stacked in bookshops.

On the back of the half-title page, the author's previous books may be listed. This is called an *ad card*. Illustrated books sometimes use the back of the half-title page for an illustration known as a *frontispiece*. Sometimes books are designed so that this page forms a double-page spread with the *title page*.

Title page: Every book has a title page, and it contains some of the most important information about the book. Both sides of the leaf are considered to be part of the title page. The front page includes the full official title of the book, including a subtitle (if there is one); names of people associated with the creation of the book, such as the author, illustrator, adaptor, editor, or translator; an editorial imprint; and the name of the company that published the book. The title page sometimes includes the year of publication and information about the edition.

The **copyright page** is often chock-full of small print that reveals a great deal about the book. The copyright information usually appears after the title page, but in some books it is placed at the end of the book, usually on the final page. The year of original publication is shown in the copyright date, which follows the symbol ©. Referring to the copyright statement should be part of every critic's routine because it helps to establish a context for the book you are about to evaluate. Was the book originally published in another country or in an earlier edition? If so, the copyright page will tell you. When more than one date is listed in the copyright line, the one that corresponds to the book you are holding in your hand is always the most recent year. This is the date you will cite in the bibliographic information accompanying your review.

Publishers generally include information related to a book's printing history on the copyright page. People sometimes use the terms *printing* and *edition* interchangeably; however, they are technically not the same thing. *Edition* refers to all the copies of a book printed from the same set of files. There may be several *printings* of a single edition but, except for occasional minor changes such as the correction of a misspelling, there are not significant textual differences between printings. You may see a notation on the copyright page such as *First Edition*, which generally means the book you are holding is the first printing of the first edition, in other words the first appearance of this particular text. The notation *First American Edition* is often a sign that the book was previously published in another country. When that is the case, you may see a statement beginning with the words "First published in . . ." which will tell you the country of origin, the date of first publication, and the original publisher of the book. If parts of the book were first published elsewhere (such as in a magazine), as is often the case with collections of poetry and short stories, this should be indicated on the copyright page as well, or on a continuation of that page.

Many publishers also include a printing code here, showing the number of printings a particular edition of a book has been through. In printing codes, the numerals from 1 through 10 may run backward or forward or may show the even numbers running forward, followed by the odd numbers running backward. Whichever way the numbers appear, the lowest one that appears in the code tells you the number of the printing of the book you are holding.

For example, 2 4 6 8 10 9 7 5 3 1 is a standard code for a first printing. Note that the lowest number in this string is 1—that's how we can tell the book is a first printing. Using the same style of code, a fourth printing would be 4 6 8 10 9 7 5. The numerals 1, 2, and 3 have been dropped from this string. Another publisher might designate a first printing with 10 9 8 7 6 5 4 3 2 1 and a fourth printing as 10 9 8 7 6 5 4.

Today most books published in the United States also include *Library of Congress Cataloging-in-Publication data* (CIP) on the copyright page.

The CIP data has the sort of information that is used in a library catalog and includes the book's author; title; ISBNs; subject headings; library classification; and, for children's books, a one- or two-line summary of the book. Like the dust jacket, the CIP data should never be taken as an integral part of the book. The book creators have no control over this information; therefore, books should never be criticized for misinformation in the CIP data. The *International Standard Book Number* (ISBN) is an important piece of information that appears here (and usually above the bar code on the back of the jacket or cover); each binding of each title has a unique ISBN, to be used in placing orders to purchase it. Trade bindings, library bindings, and paperback editions of the same books all have separate ISBNs, which should be indicated in every review's bibliographic citation.

Other valuable details related to a book's production are sometimes found on the copyright page. You may find, for example, an author's source note for a folktale. If photographs have been used to illustrate the book, photo credits often appear here. In picture books some publishers now indicate the illustration media on the copyright page and, in books of all kinds, names and sizes of type styles used may be cited, in addition to the name of the book designer.

The next recto page often consists of the author's and artist's *dedications* of the work to one or more individuals. Like jacket art, flap copy, and CIP data summaries, dedications are generally irrelevant to the assessment of the book as a whole.

Sometimes an author thanks someone who has been helpful in the book's creation, and this sort of information should be included in the *acknowledgments page*, which sometimes follows the dedication page or sometimes appears at the end of the book. Unlike dedications, acknowledgments can be significant to the critic: It is quite common for writers to seek out the expert opinions of content specialists who read over the final manuscript of a book prior to publication and point out any inaccuracies or implausibilities they notice. This sort of acknowledgment by the author usually indicates the content specialist's professional affiliation. Phillip Hoose's book *The Race to Save the Lord God Bird* includes in his acknowledgments:

> *Many scientists, including Dr. Davis Finch and Dr. David Wilcove, helped me evaluate facts and ideas and led me to materials concerning everything from grubs to extinction. Dr. Larry Master, Chief Zoologist for NatureServe, read much of the scientific material critically and saved me from embarrassing errors.*

This shows that even though the author is trained as a scientist himself, he sought out the opinions of others who were experts in the field, and it may be of help in assessing accuracy.

Preface: A short note, written by the author, includes details about the creation of the book that are not an essential part of the book's content. Sometimes called simply an *author's note*, it may give readers a brief description of what inspired the author to write the book, or it may tell us why the author believes the subject of the book is important. In children's books, we sometimes see a variant of this called "A Note to Parents." This typically includes information about the levels of understanding children are likely to possess at different ages. For example, Robie H. Harris's book about human reproduction, *It's Not the Stork*, includes a note for parents and other adults working with young children outlining the types of questions young children have about the subject and suggests how best to use the book with them.

Foreword: Like the preface, a foreword is also a short note about the book's creation and the need for information on the topic; however, a foreword is generally written by someone other than the author, often an expert on the book's subject.

Contents: Books with chapter headings include a table of contents that lists the front matter, part title headings, chapter headings, and back matter in order and indicates the page number for the beginning of each. The contents can be especially helpful in a nonfiction book because it often reveals the organization (or lack thereof) of the material in the book. In novels, chapter titles listed in the contents can provide a quick summary of the action, which can help you remember plot details after you have read the book.

Between the contents and the body of the book, the publisher may insert another *half-title page*. If the book is divided into two or more named parts, there will be a *part-title page* right before the beginning of the body of the book. This may simply say "Part One" or "Book One," or it might give a specific title to the section, such as "The Escape."

BACK MATTER

Additional information often appears at the end of the book, particularly in works of nonfiction. Back matter can be an essential part of the book, and it should be evaluated and reviewed as carefully as the body of the book itself.

Epilogue: A brief concluding statement that stands apart from the text as a whole. There is often a sense that the author has made a sudden jump ahead in time from the body of the book. Margot Theis Raven's picture book *Let Them Play*, illustrated by Chris Ellison, recounts a 1955 World Series Little League game in which an all-black team was not allowed to play. A one-page epilogue fast-forwards to 2002, when the original team members, now old men, took a bus to the opening ceremonies of the Little League World Series, where they were presented with a championship banner.

Afterword: A short and usually subjective passage in which the author shares his or her own personal responses related to the subject of the book. At the end of *Hitler Youth: Growing Up in Hitler's Shadow,* author Susan Campbell Bartoletti tells readers:

> *This book is my attempt to understand the role of young people during a devastating twelve-year period of history that changed our world forever. It is my attempt to make sense out of the fact that adults taught young people to hate, to kill, and to feel superior over others. After all, the Hitler Youth weren't born Nazis; they became Nazis.*

Appendix: Supplementary material on a particular aspect of a nonfiction topic is sometimes included in an organized section at the back of the book. A book on the history of major-league baseball, for example, might include an appendix providing a chronological listing of World Series winners. Appendices are typically labeled by letters A, B, C, and so on, followed by a descriptive title:

Appendix A: World Series Winners

Appendix B: All-time Record Holders

Glossary: An alphabetical list of words and/or expressions used in the body of the book that may be unfamiliar to readers. Each entry in a glossary is defined, and sometimes a pronunciation is included. Glossaries are usually confined to the special vocabulary related to the subject of the book. A book on a ballet company, for instance, might include a glossary of words such as "arabesque," "barre," and "pointe." A book written in English but that includes some words and expressions in Spanish might have a glossary that gives the definitions and pronunciations of the Spanish used in the text.

Source notes: In nonfiction, *source notes,* or *references,* provide readers with a record of the original sources the author consulted while researching the topic. Source notes are usually listed chapter by chapter, in the order in which the information is cited in the text. Authors sometimes include a sentence or two that gives readers insight into the research process used and how decisions were made when sources conflicted with each other.

Bibliography: The original sources consulted by the author are generally listed alphabetically by the author in a bibliography. In books for the young, authors sometimes provide "Books for Further Reading," a list of books on the subject that are written at roughly the same age level as the book in hand.

Index: An alphabetical list of topics and/or names that appear in the body of the book, accompanied by the page numbers on which the items can be found.

Bio: Biographical information about the author sometimes appears on the last page of the book. This may be a restatement of the back flap bio, or it may be an expanded version.

CATEGORIES OF CHILDREN'S BOOKS

We typically categorize children's books in two ways: by *age level* and by *genre*, or type. Juvenile trade publishing produces books for all ages of children, from babies up through the teen years. The age level of the intended audience generally dictates both form and content.

Nonfiction, or books of information as they are often called, is published for all ages. But two books on the same topic, even written by the same author, will be very different from each other if one is aimed at three-year-olds and the other is written for children from ages eight to ten. It stands to reason that a book on human reproduction published for preschoolers will differ greatly from a book on the same subject published for adolescents. The age level of the intended audience may also dictate subject matter. A book on going to day care would obviously be for preschoolers, and a book on the history of the Negro Baseball Leagues, for older readers.

Folklore and *poetry* are also published for all ages of children. As with nonfiction, both style and content will differ according to the age levels of the intended audience. Many picture-book editions of single folktales are published every year, some for children as young as two or three and some for children as old as eight or nine. Collections of folktales and other kinds of traditional literature, such as mythology, tall tales, and epic literature, are generally aimed at school-age children. Young children, who respond naturally to rhythm and rhyme, are a receptive audience for nursery rhymes and humorous verse, the early roots of poetry. Older children enjoy humorous verse as well, in addition to more sophisticated forms of true poetry, some of which is especially written for children and some selected from poetry written for adults.

In the area of *fiction*, we get a clearer breakdown by age level, as specific forms of fiction have been created to meet the unique needs and interests of children at various ages. *Picture books* have been especially developed as an art form with young children in mind. These thirty-two-page creations ingeniously combine words and pictures to tell stories preschoolers want to hear again and again. *Easy readers* are the next step up from picture books. They are consciously created to help build the skills of children who are just learning to read. *Transitional books* move up one step more to serve as a bridge between easy readers and children's novels, often called *chapter books*. At all levels, children's fiction covers a range of subjects, themes, and styles and represents some of the best writing we find in the world of literature today.

In the upcoming chapters, we will take a closer look at all these categories. Each one merits special consideration and requires a slightly different approach. Since this book is intended for people who are new to the field of children's books, I will provide a brief history of the different types of children's books as they have developed in U.S. trade publishing so that you can get a sense of how these books came to be. In discussing critical standards, I will use examples from well-known and easily available books that also represent some of the best books of their type. I recommend that you seek out any of these books that you don't know so that you can read them to build your familiarity with the literature.

Throughout the book, I will suggest questions you can ask yourself as you go on to evaluate books on your own. These questions are intended not as a test but to help you begin to make concrete critical judgments about what you are reading. Some of the questions may already seem obvious to you. If so, that's good! You are well on your way to being a critical reader and a responsible reviewer. As you gain experience with book evaluation, these sorts of questions will become second nature to you.

Finally, there is no substitute for reading widely yourself. The more experience you have as a reader of children's books, the easier it will be for you to think about the one you have just read. One of the most important skills you can acquire is the ability to place a book in an appropriate context. How does it measure up against others of its type? *Are* there, in fact, others of its type? Or is this something fresh and new? One of the greatest thrills for a children's book reviewer is to find the book that is truly innovative and groundbreaking, or completely satisfying and close to perfect. That's what keeps us all reading.

CHAPTER 2

Books of Information

Nonfiction is an essential part of every child's library, whether the child reads it for specific information, recreation, or both. Many children prefer to read nonfiction exclusively, and they may voraciously read every children's book a library owns on the subject of horses or ancient Egypt or basketball. Young readers sometimes go through phases during which they will read only biographies, for example, or books about dinosaurs. Some children like to browse through highly visual books of information, pausing to read captions and perhaps a bit of corresponding text when a picture grabs their attention. Others trek to the library, looking for books on a particular topic they have been assigned to report on at school. Whatever their motivation for reading nonfiction, children deserve to have books of information that are accurate, engaging, and well written.

The past few decades have seen great changes in children's nonfiction, many of which may be traced to the mid-1980s. Nonfiction languished throughout the 1970s, due to cuts in federal funding that previously had supported school library purchases of nonfiction (science in particular), then made a comeback after several titles were cited as Newbery Honor Books. The impact of the Newbery Medal cannot be underestimated in contemporary children's literature published in the United States. Because the Newbery Medal has a tremendous impact on sales, it continues to set the standard for excellence in children's books. It also seems to have an impact on what sorts of books get published. Unfortunately, the Newbery Committee rarely honors nonfiction, a fact that was brought to the public's attention in 1976 by Milton Meltzer's widely read *Horn Book* essay, "Where Do All the Prizes Go?: The Case for Nonfiction."

Although the Newbery Committee had recognized nonfiction prior to this time—in fact, the first Newbery was awarded in 1922 to a non-fiction book, *The Story of Mankind*, by Hendrik Willem van Loon—it was not until the mid-1980s that the honors came more frequently. In 1984, *Sugaring Time*, by Kathryn Lasky with photographs by Christopher G. Knight, won a Newbery Honor. In 1986 the Newbery Committee named Rhoda Blumberg's *Commodore Perry in the Land of the Shogun* as an Honor Book; and in 1987, a science book, *Volcano: The Eruption and Healing of Mount St. Helens*, by Patricia Lauber, was cited as such. Finally in 1988 the Newbery Medal was awarded to a nonfiction book for the first time in more than thirty years—to Russell Freedman's *Lincoln: A Photobiography*.

While there has always been excellent nonfiction published for children, these four books stood out not only for their distinguished writing but also for their eye-catching presentations. *Volcano*, for example, was one of the first photo-essays to use color photographs. Today, it would be hard to find a children's photo-essay that didn't. *Lincoln* was gener-ously illustrated, so much so that the word "photobiography" was used to call attention to this fact in the book's subtitle, lest potential readers dismiss the book as just another dull, thick black-and-white biography. Since 1988, there have been many biographies for children that imitate the look of Freedman's book by using dozens of photographs to illustrate the text.

All these books stand out as examples representing two forces at work: the American population, including both children and adults, was being seen as more visually oriented—that is, more responsive to pictures than printed words—and changes in technology allowed publishers to cater to this belief. Almost overnight we began to see newspapers and magazines decrease the number of printed words and increase the numbers of illustrations. In publications for children, this trend had the biggest impact on nonfiction. We began to see books of information that relied more on illustration, with many book creators successfully using unconventional approaches in presenting information to children. The books in Joanna Cole and Bruce Degen's innovative series the Magic School Bus were pioneers in this area. Their trademark style of combining fact and fiction, using multiple strands of narrative and healthy doses of humor, has been widely imitated in books of information.

The 1980s also saw a change in attitudes toward fictionalization in children's nonfiction. In earlier decades, it was considered perfectly acceptable for authors writing biographies to invent scenes and dialogue. But biographer Jean Fritz set a new standard for children's nonfiction writers with her highly acclaimed biographies for young readers: Fritz didn't include dialogue unless she could document that her subject had actually said it, showing that it was possible to write lively, engaging biographies without fictionalization. "I don't make up facts, but at the same time I have no desire to write in a factual style," Fritz wrote about her work in 1988. "Nonfiction can be told in a narrative voice and still maintain integrity. The art of fiction is making up facts; the art of nonfiction is using facts to make up a form."

Another change introduced at around the same time was that

nonfiction was now being aimed at younger and younger children. Books of information are regularly published for preschoolers, some for children as young as two years old. This suggests a conscious move away from the idea that nonfiction books are mostly "homework" books. Interestingly, some small children, like their older peers, show a definite preference for books of information or "books with real stuff," as they call them. Others just as happily accept both kinds of books, if their adults are open-minded enough to offer them nonfiction as well as storybooks. And a lot of books of information for preschoolers serve a dual purpose and function as a bridge between adult and child, informing two generations simultaneously. *A Baby's Coming to Your House!*, by Shelley Moore Thomas, with photographs by Eric Futran, provides young children with basic information about what it's like to live with a newborn, while it also lets parents know what sorts of concerns and questions older preschool-age siblings are likely to have.

Since 1988, there have been a handful of nonfiction Newbery Honor Books, including three more highly visual biographies by Russell Freedman. But, as Jonathan Hunt points out in reassessment of the nonfiction landscape in "Where Do All the Prizes Go?: Thoughts on the State of Informational Books," thirty years after Meltzer's article first appeared, nonfiction still appears to be a neglected genre, as far as the Newbery Medal is concerned. That does not appear to be the case with the Caldecott; in the same time period, there have been three Caldecott Medal winners that are categorized as nonfiction: *Snowflake Bentley*, by Jacqueline Briggs Martin, illustrated by Mary Azarian; *So You Want to Be President*, by Judith St. George, illustrated by David Small; and *The Man Who Walked Between the Towers*, by Mordicai Gerstein, as well as several that were Caldecott Honor Books. Hunt attributes this to the fact that we are living in a "golden age of informational picture books." He also traces the problem to the criteria the

Newbery Committee must use that does not allow them to consider illustrations unless they detract from the text. For children's nonfiction, which today relies heavily on illustration as well as text to get information across, this would cause the committee to rule out most of the outstanding books of information.

Perhaps with these sorts of concerns in mind, the Association for Library Service to Children responsible for overseeing the Newbery and Caldecott awards established a new award for nonfiction in 2001 called the Robert F. Sibert Informational Book Medal. In selecting the winning books each year, the committee considers both text and illustrations, in recognition of the importance of the visual elements in nonfiction books. This award, along with the Orbis Pictus Award for Outstanding Nonfiction for Children, established by the National Council of Teachers of English in 1990, gave greater visibility to the genre overall and raised the standards of excellence in children's informational books.

With all the variety in approach and content found in these books of information—not to mention the needs, abilities, and interests of the young readers themselves—there are still critical standards that can be applied across the board in the evaluation of children's nonfiction. You need not be a subject specialist yourself (though it helps!) to evaluate them, but you do need to be a careful and critical reader. Approach the book with a questioning mind as you think about its accuracy, organization, illustrations, design, prose, and documentation.

AUTHORITY AND RESPONSIBILITY OF THE AUTHOR

The first question to ask yourself as you approach a book of information is: Who is the author? It may be a name you know and recognize as a reputable writer of information books for children, or it may be a name you have never seen before.

Check for an author bio at the back of the book or on the back flap to try to determine what sort of authority the author has. You might recognize the name Sid Fleischman as a writer of children's novels, for example, but until you read the flap copy of *Escape! The Story of the Great Houdini*, you might not know that he was trained as a magician, a fact that gives him special insight into the subject of his book. Biographical information often reveals that an author has an educational background related to the subject about which he or she is writing. This is not to say that an author *must* have formal education in a particular field in order to write about it; it is merely the first step the responsible critic takes in a systematic evaluation of a book's accuracy. By the same token, you must not assume that an author's subject expertise guarantees success in writing for children, even if he or she has written outstanding children's nonfiction in the past. Again, an assessment of the author's authority is just one piece of critical information you may use in building your evaluation of a book.

Check the acknowledgments next to see if the author has cited the name of a content specialist who read the manuscript for accuracy. This is an especially important step for writers who do not have a background in the subject about which they are writing, and even those who do often wisely seek the informed opinion of another expert. The children's nonfiction writer often walks a fine line between making a subject comprehensible to children and simplifying to the point of inaccuracy. A content specialist can call an author's attention to areas in which he or she is in danger of having crossed into the realm of inaccuracy. Beyond assuring accuracy, the acknowledgment of expert advice shows that the author respects young readers and believes it is important that they have access to accurate information.

Another indication that the nonfiction writer respects the needs of young readers is the use of inclusive language and illustrations. By this we mean that boys *and* girls of all racial backgrounds should feel included, rather than excluded, from the social life of the book. Both text and illustrations should show a realistic diversity of different types of people. An excellent example of how an author's or illustrator's responsible choices in this area enhance the material is *Hominids: A Look Back at Our Ancestors*, by Helen Roney Sattler, illustrated by Christopher Santoro. Both the author and illustrator have avoided the white male bias that has been prevalent in studies of human evolution for decades simply by taking a broader—and more realistic—view of the human family. Beginning with the use of the anthropologically accurate term "hominid" instead of the popular term "early man," Sattler is careful to use language that specifies gender only when gender is significant in her discussion (the height of a female *Australopithecus afarensis* versus that of her male counterpart). Similarly, Santoro's black-and-white line drawings show males and females in equal number; and when drawing comparisons between ancient hominids and contemporary humans, people of all races are shown as the norm.

Of course, there will be instances in nonfiction when the subject matter dictates that only one race or gender be represented. One would not expect to see women gratuitously included, for example, among the signers of the U.S. Declaration of Independence nor would one expect to see Norwegians present during the construction of the Great Wall of China. But the vast majority of topics covered in the field of children's nonfiction can be approached with a wide vision. There is no excuse in this day and age for a children's book of science experiments, for example, to show only white boys with test tubes.

ORGANIZATION

The way in which information is organized in books for young readers is of the utmost importance. A good nonfiction book arranges material in a logical sequence. The two most common organizational patterns in books of information for children are *enumeration* and *chronological order.*

In enumeration the author describes the relevant parts of a subject in some sort of orderly fashion. *Little Lions, Bull Baiters & Hunting Hounds: A History of Dog Breeds,* by Jeff Crosby and Shelley Ann Jackson, describes forty-three different dog breeds that are arranged in four broad categories: hunting breeds, herding breeds, working breeds, and companion breeds. Within each broad category there are subcategories. Hunting breeds, for example, includes sight hounds, scent hounds, sporting breeds, and terriers.

Chronological order is the obvious pattern for history or biography, but not all books using chronological order follow a straight line from past to present. In *Who Was First? Discovering the Americas,* Russell Freedman uses reverse chronological order, beginning with Christopher Columbus and moving back through time to explore accounts of Chinese travelers in the early 1400s to Leif Eriksson in 1000 A.D. to archaeological evidence of human activity in Brazil dating back 50,000 years. Freedman's approach gives young readers a sense of historical method, and that scientific theories are not always in agreement. Karen Levine combines two alternating chronologies in *Hana's Suitcase.* The first gives an account of a Holocaust museum curator in Tokyo who from 2000 to 2001 worked to track down the owner of a child's suitcase that had been donated to them by the Auschwitz Museum. The second traces the short life of the suitcase's owner, Hana Brady, a Jewish child who had lived during the Holocaust. Each of the alternating narratives provides a dramatic tension for the other until they converge with the revelation that Hana did not survive but that her brother did and was still alive.

Before you begin to read any nonfiction book, you should look at it critically to see how it is organized. In longer books of nonfiction, a table of contents often provides a clear picture of a book's organization. Take, for example, the table of contents in Stephen Krensky's *Comic Book Century: The History of American Comic Books*:

Introduction
Superheroes Take Off
The Comics Go to War
Thriving on the Home Front
Comics under Fire
A New Era
Going Underground
Looking Forward and Back
The World Turned Upside Down
Epilogue

Even without dates cited, we can ascertain that his book is arranged chronologically. Now let's take the chapter headings in Catherine Thimmesh's excellent account of the 1974 discovery of what was then the oldest known human ancestor, *Lucy Long Ago: Uncovering the Mystery of Where We Came From*:

It
Child or Grownup?
Boy or Girl?
Known Species or New?
Ancient or Modern?
Wobbling or Walking?
Image?
Lucy

Just by looking at the chapter titles, you can see a logical order in Thimmesh's arrangement of her subject matter, beginning with the discovery of a fossil skeleton that so completely flummoxed paleontologists, it could only be thought of as "it." From there, Thimmesh presents the sorts of questions the discovery raised, beginning with the most elemental ones about age and gender, then moving on to more complex questions about where the skeleton fit in the context of evolution, and ending with a more fleshed out identity. Each chapter follows the scientific methods used to answer the questions posed, thus providing readers with a sense of how science works in addition to the answers.

Many shorter books for young children have a straight narrative that is not broken up into chapters. That doesn't necessarily mean the books lack logical organization. A common pattern in books of information for young children is to begin with the familiar and move to the unfamiliar. A book for young children on the subject of tigers, for example, might start out with house cats, an animal familiar to most children, and then move by extension to the less familiar animal, tigers. This technique takes into account what children are likely to know at a particular age and uses their common knowledge as a foundation. The opening paragraph of *Sisters & Brothers: Sibling Relationships in the Animal World*, by Steve Jenkins and Robin Page, provides a good example:

> *Playing together, working together, arguing, fighting—sometimes animal brothers and sisters act a lot like human siblings. Other creatures have more unusual relationships. They may be identical quadruplets, or have only sisters. Some have hundreds, thousands, or even millions of brothers and sisters. There are animal brothers that fight to the death, and others that are companions for life. In this book you can read about some of the ways animal siblings get along—or not.*

Each subsequent double-page spread in the book is labeled to show the characteristic it demonstrates: one at a time, quadruplets, sisters, a large family, a very large family, competition, sibling rivalry, playing games, learning together, living together, working together, cooperating, staying together, stepsisters and stepbrothers, only child. Note that even though each page can be looked at as a self-contained whole, there is still a logical progression from one characteristic to the next.

A clear logical sequence can also be seen in Gail Gibbons's easy picture books about different sports written for very young readers, *My Baseball Book*, *My Basketball Book*, *My Football Book*, and *My Soccer Book*. Even though every volume deals with a different sport, each one follows the same order:

Equipment
Playing field
Object of the game
Number of players on a team
Player positions
Length of the game
How a game starts
What happens in a game
How teams score
Rules and penalties
Breaks in the game
How play resumes after a break
How the game ends

Whenever you set out to evaluate a book of information you should always try to get a sense of the book's distinct parts and how they are related to one another—in other words, how the information is organized.

Shorter works that are not divided into chapters might have internal headings that will set off the various parts of the text. The distinct parts should, at the very least, be clear to you as you are reading the book; if they're not, this is likely an indication that the author has not succeeded in clearly organizing the material for a young audience.

One final type of organization of the book's material is with an alphabetical index that appears at the end of the book. Good indexes give readers access to specific pieces of information within the body of the text.

ILLUSTRATIONS

When the winners of the first Sibert Medal were announced in 2001, many were pleasantly surprised with the inclusion of a graphic novel, *Pedro and Me: Friendship, Loss, and What I Learned*, by Judd Winick. Using the conventions of a comic book, cartoonist Judd Winick told the moving story of his experiences as part of the cast of MTV's *The Real World: San Francisco*, when he was assigned a roommate named Pedro Zamora, who was gay and HIV-positive. Getting to know Pedro changed Winick's life, and his book-length comic provides the perfect vehicle for his seriocomic account of their friendship.

Since the publication of *Pedro and Me* we have begun to see a steady stream of graphic novels aimed at teens and, more recently, at children. Those that fall into the nonfiction category are among the best of the genre, and they range from a candid memoir of a young ballet dancer in *To Dance: A Memoir* to a dramatic visual account of a single escape made by Harry Houdini in *Houdini: The Handcuff King*. The speed with which graphic novels have taken hold in the children's book industry and their increasing popularity with children and teens is perhaps a testament to a growing recognition of the needs and interests of visual learners.

As traditional children's nonfiction has become more and more visual in recent years, illustrations have become a more essential part of the overall structure. Indeed, many of the finest books of information engage young readers by asking them to look for some specific thing in an accompanying photograph or drawing, encouraging interplay between the text and illustrations. In Sally M. Walker's *Written in Bone: Buried Lives of Jamestown and Colonial Maryland*, dozens of photographs of skeletal remains from an archaeological dig in Jamestown draw the readers' attention to notable features, such as semicircular grooves in a man's teeth and a large piece of broken pottery lying unceremoniously on top of a boy's skeleton. Here the illustrations are not only being used to illustrate the text but also to draw children into the scientific process by showing that scientists formulate theories from observations.

Color photographs are being used today in a great number of science books to convey information that would be otherwise inaccessible. Seymour Simon has used the extraordinary photographs made available by NASA expeditions in recent years in his books about the solar system, such as *Destination: Jupiter*. NASA photographs of landscapes from Mars are placed side by side with photos taken in the Atacama Desert in Chile to show their similarities in *Life on Earth and Beyond: An Astrobiologist's Quest*, by Pamela S. Turner. The Atacama Desert is just one of the extreme environments featured here in text and photographs; and whether they were taken here on Earth or on Mars, they give children views of places to which they wouldn't otherwise have access. Nic Bishop uses high-speed photography and extreme close-ups in books such as *Red-Eyed Tree Frog* and *Spiders* to make it possible for children to see small creatures and observe behaviors that would be impossible to observe in their natural settings.

Recent advances in photo reproduction have opened the door to a popular subgenre of children's nonfiction: the photo-essay. These books combine text and photographs to give readers a you-are-there sense and cover a wide range of subjects from a typical day in the life of the raptor rescue center in St. Paul, Minnesota, to the contrasting lives of a Palestinian boy and Jewish boy living in Jerusalem. Author-photographer Susan Kuklin has set the standard for excellence in this genre. Since 1984 she has produced photo-essays on a wide variety of topics for children from preschool through the teen years; all are based on primary research through interviews and observation, documented by her photographs. In *Families*, for example, she combines color photographs with first-person statements from children living in different kinds of families. Kuklin chooses her subjects carefully so that they represent her topic, and yet she always allows for enough diversity that a single person does not carry the responsibility for representing everyone. Houghton Mifflin's series Scientists in the Field uses the photo-essay technique to document the work of different kinds of scientists while at the same time providing information about the science itself. *The Mysterious Universe: Supernovae, Dark Energy, and Black Holes*, by Ellen Jackson, with photographs and illustrations by Nic Bishop, follows astronomy professor Alex Filippenko on a research trip to the Keck Observatory atop an inactive volcano in Hawaii as accompanying text offers an introduction to Dr. Filippenko's area of expertise: dark energy.

Color reproduction in books has become so sophisticated lately that it is quite easy to be bowled over by a book's dazzling illustrations. It is important, however, not to lose sight of the main purpose of illustrations in a book of information: to provide information by complementing, supporting, or extending the text. Look closely at a book's illustrations to determine what exactly they add to the work. How do they relate to the text? Are they merely decorative, or do they actually enhance the text in some way? Do they make the subject matter more appealing? Are they up-to-date? Are captions clear and accurate? Do the captions add supplementary information or repeat what's in the text?

DESIGN

We often speak of book design in terms of overall aesthetic appeal, but when it comes to nonfiction, design becomes an important aspect of getting information across to readers. In addition to making the subject seem more inviting, the design of a nonfiction book can be used to clarify the sequence of ideas and to show how the parts are related. Headings and subheadings can be set in different type sizes and styles to illuminate the organization of ideas.

Loree Griffin Burns's *Tracking Trash: Flotsam, Jetsam, and the Science of Ocean Motion* integrates two simultaneous narratives, one that describes the scientist at work and the other, the science itself. Two distinct styles of typography clearly distinguish the two from each other. In addition, the historical background that opens each chapter and the photo captions are also highlighted in different typographic styles. Thanks to design, the points of reference are always clear to young readers.

Design is a big factor in the success of the Magic School Bus series by Joanna Cole and Bruce Degen. Open to any page in a book from this series and note the various strands of information operating simultaneously through text, dialogue, and student reports. In *The Magic School Bus Lost in the Solar System*, for example, a fourth strand is introduced with the teacher Ms. Frizzle occasionally reading from her lesson plans; this is clearly marked off from other dialogue simply through the use of pink lined paper as the background of her dialogue bubbles. There is a lot going on on every page of the books in this series. An innovative design allows not only for this to make perfect sense but also for the story to function as science and fantasy at the same time.

Candace Fleming excels at creating outstanding works of nonfiction about history using what she terms a scrapbook style. These highly visual volumes are arranged by themes and topics; and each double-page spread includes photographs, drawings, and short bursts of text that provide a context for the illustrative material. *The Lincolns: A Scrapbook Look at Abraham and Mary* uses only one style of typography throughout, carefully selected to add historical authenticity; but on any given page, each piece stands out thanks to an exceptional design that uses boxes, bars, borders, banners, headings, and subheadings. The design here has two functions: it provides unity and clarity for the disparate pieces of text and illustration, and it gives a sense of the time period in which the Lincolns lived by using typographical conventions of the mid-nineteenth century.

A fully integrated, successful design does not call attention to itself, so the critical reader must look closely at all the elements of book design to see how they work. Look first at the typography. Is the type size appropriate for the intended audience? Children are very sensitive to the size of a book's type. Large type and shorter line length make text more readable for children in third and fourth grades; but by the time a child is in fifth grade, large type signals that the book is for "babies" and no self-respecting fifth grader would be caught dead with it. These same children are put off, however, by a sea of type; a medium-sized typeface with lots of white space on each page seems to suit them best.

In addition to type size, look at the type style. Are different styles used consistently to get across different kinds of information? If headings and subheadings are used, do they appear in different type styles, or are subheadings bulleted or indented to set them off from headings?

Look at the placement of illustrations. Do they generally appear next to the text that discusses what they picture, or do readers have to do a lot of flipping back and forth to match text with pictures? Do the illustrations frequently break up the flow of the text, or do they enhance it?

WRITING STYLE

While background research, organization and structure, design and illustrations are all used to present information to children, writing style ultimately brings the subject to life. Clear prose that engages the reader, stirs the imagination, and awakens the mind is every bit as important in works of nonfiction as it is in fiction. When the author has a passion for the subject matter, that enthusiasm is transferred to the reader through his or her writing style.

Laurence Pringle is a master at writing dynamic prose in his science books for children. By doing so, he makes his subject matter more interesting by demonstrating the nature of scientific inquiry—or what many writers refer to as the "scientific attitude."

Consider the way he opens *Alligators and Crocodiles! Strange and Wonderful*, an introduction to crocodilians for very young children:

> *Erk, erk, erk. Erk, erk, erk, erk.*
>
> *Baby alligators called to their mother. They called from inside their eggs, which she had buried within a mound of grasses and other plants. For more than two months, the mother alligator had guarded the eggs in the nest. Now about forty baby alligators were ready to hatch.*
>
> *Erk, erk, erk, the babies called. Where was their mother?*

Pringle uses the drama inherent in the natural world to capture children's attention. In just a few short sentences, he provides quite a bit of information about alligators: They lay eggs; they build nests on the ground out of grasses and other plants; it takes two months for the eggs to hatch, during which time the mother guards the nest; they have about forty hatchlings; and when the babies are ready to hatch, they call to their mother. In spite of the simplicity of the language Pringle uses, he does not talk down to his young readers. His tone shows that he has respect for their intelligence.

Pringle enlivens his prose by using a conversational tone that is made up of everyday language, includes questions, and occasionally addresses the reader directly by using the second person. The author's mood toward both subject and audience is expressed through tone. In nonfiction, we see a range of tones used successfully.

As Pringle demonstrates, a conversational tone is frequently used in books of information for young children. It appears less frequently in books for older readers. However, Kadir Nelson used a conversational tone ingeniously in *We Are the Ship: The Story of Negro League Baseball*:

> *By the late 1800s, Negroes began to disappear from professional baseball teams and were soon gone from them altogether. Now, there was never any written rule that prohibited Negroes from playing professional baseball, but soon after 1887, somehow Negroes all over couldn't get on a professional baseball team. Come to find out that all the white owners had gotten together in secret and decided to do away with Negroes in professional baseball. They agreed not to add any more to their teams and to let go of the ones they had. Called it a "gentleman's agreement." And I'll tell you this, the white pro-ball-club owners held to that agreement for sixty years.*

Nelson's conversational tone gives readers the sense that they are hearing the history recounted by one of the old-timers who experienced it all firsthand, a device that really brings the history to life as it brings readers closer to the subject.

A humorous tone is the hallmark of Joanna Cole's Magic School Bus books and is employed brilliantly as well in Sid Fleischman's *The Trouble Begins at 8: A Life of Mark Twain in the Wild, Wild West*:

> At the same time, Clemens reacted with dismay at the gross humbugability of his fellow man. This judgment would agitate his sensibilities until he petrified into a public scold. So ruffled did he become at the human gift for homespun ignorance and hypocrisy, for greed and crackpot bigotry, that he would become a one-man firing squad.
>
> "Our Heavenly Father invented man because he was disappointed in the monkey," he declared.
>
> "If you pick up a starving dog and make him prosperous, he will not bite you. That is the principal difference between a dog and a man."

Fleischman's bombastic prose, with its frequent hyperbole and clever turns of phrase, pays homage to Twain's own witty style.

Unfortunately, in lesser hands, attempts at a humorous tone in informational books for children fall flat, and the books end up sounding condescending or just plain silly. But when authors know their subjects well and have respect for the intelligence of their audience, a humorous tone can add a great deal of appeal to a book of information.

Sally M. Walker's book *Secrets of a Civil War Submarine: Solving the Mysteries of the H. L. Hunley* uses a neutral tone by presenting its information matter-of-factly, as can be seen in the following example:

> As Owsley assessed the bones' visible features, he saw no evidence of physical trauma that would indicate that the crew had struggled during an attempt to escape from the submarine. As the

archaeologists had surmised from the locations and positions of some
of the remains, it appeared that the men had died in or near their
assigned stations.

Note the precision and clarity of Walker's language as she presents and interprets evidence from the 130-year-old wreck. Her use of words such as "surmised" and "appeared" provides a constant reminder of the theoretical nature of history and science. It also signals a distinction between fact and informed opinion, and demonstrates the nature of true scholarship.

An author who cares deeply about his or her subject matter may take a partisan tone in nonfiction. In his powerful social histories for young readers, Milton Meltzer is known and respected for the strong partisan tone he takes. Writing about his book *Never to Forget: The Jews of the Holocaust*, he comments: "Terrible and complex as the events were, they can be brought within the range of understanding if the reader is helped to see them from the inside. If a reader can be made to feel, to care, he or she will be much more ready to understand."

Walter Dean Myers skillfully uses matter-of-fact descriptions of historical events to support and explain his partisan tone in *Now Is Your Time! The African-American Struggle for Freedom*:

What was it like to be called a slave? What was it like to be "owned"
by someone? There is no single answer to this question. There is the
common experience of being considered inferior, of being bought and
sold as if one were a horse or household furniture. Many people who
sold Africans would often add a few household items to the sale so
that they did not appear to be "slave dealers." Most plantation own-
ers did not seem to realize that the Africans hated the very idea of
not being free. (George Washington, in August of 1761, complained

that his Africans ran away without cause.) But the best way to find out what it was like to spend a lifetime in bondage is to read the documents from those days.

Myers then goes on to present primary evidence from firsthand accounts written in the nineteenth century in reports, letters, reminiscences, and business statements, allowing readers to, in Milton Meltzer's terms, "see them from the inside."

More recently, Tanya Lee Stone's *Almost Astronauts: 13 Women Who Dared to Dream* takes a partisan tone to show how strongly the author feels about the inequities suffered by women in the United States space program:

But that phrase, "before their time," gets right to the heart of the problem. Why should there ever be a particular time that's right or wrong for any group of people? It's not that the thirteen women were outsiders trying to push their way in where they didn't belong. It's that what John Glenn called the "social order" of the time shut out strong, qualified women not because they weren't capable enough but because they were women.

Like Myers, Stone tempers her partisan tone with a neutral one as she describes the training the thirteen women underwent in the early days of NASA, before they were cut from the program.

To evaluate the writing style in nonfiction, it may be helpful to ask yourself the following questions: Is the prose clear and dynamic? What kinds of words and sentences are used to get the ideas across to young readers? Does the author use a creative or original approach to the subject matter? Does the text present principles and concepts, building on a logical development of ideas, rather than merely reciting facts and figures? What sort of tone does the author use, and is it appropriate for the subject matter? Is this a book I would want to read aloud to a child or group of children?

DOCUMENTATION OF SOURCES

By documentation we generally mean a bibliography of sources that were consulted by the writer while doing background research. Documentation can also refer to footnotes or endnotes that cite sources for direct quotes and specific pieces of information.

Most bibliographies of sources that were consulted as research appear at the back of the book. Source material can be divided into two categories: primary and secondary. The use of primary sources indicates that the author has done original research, which is becoming more and more common in children's nonfiction. To do the research for her biography of Harper Lee for Viking's Up Close Author series, Kerry Madden traveled three times to Lee's hometown of Monroeville, Alabama. Harper Lee is famously private and does not grant interviews, but Madden was able to talk with many people who grew up with her, including Truman Capote's cousin who had been Lee's childhood friend. Madden was able to use other primary sources available at the Monroe County Heritage Museum and at the Old Courthouse Museum in Monroeville. In addition, she used secondary sources, such as original articles and interviews from newspapers and magazines written at the time *To Kill a Mockingbird* was first published and then made into a film version. All these sources helped her create a full portrait of a woman few have had a chance to get to know.

Photo-essays that use the photodocumentary technique are, by definition, based on primary research. The photographs themselves, in addition to personal interviews woven into the text, provide the author's documentation. One would not expect to find a bibliography of sources in this sort of photo-essay unless the author has brought in additional information from secondary sources.

Most writers of children's nonfiction rely on secondary sources, such as books and articles that have been written by others on the topic. Take a look at the sources listed in the book you are reviewing. Are they up-to-date? Do cited articles appear in popular magazines such as *National Geographic*, or do they come from scholarly sources? One of these is not necessarily superior to the other, but a critical look at sources may give you a picture of the depth of the writer's expertise in the subject.

Another type of bibliography that frequently appears in the back of children's nonfiction is a list of suggested or further reading. The titles given there are generally aimed at young readers. It is sometimes unclear whether they were sources used by the author in his or her research. Some bibliographies integrate adult and children's material; when they do, they often indicate which titles would be appropriate for young readers.

Many authors also include notes that document sources of direct quotations used in the body of the book. The practice of using footnotes, or citations that appear at the bottom of the page on which the quote appears, is rare in children's books, most likely because footnotes are considered to be more of an academic convention than part of the art of nonfiction writing for children.

Notes from the author at the back of the book seem to be a type of documentation that is aimed at both child and adult readers. Jim Murphy is known for his lively accounts of historical events that are pulled together from multiple firsthand accounts. The notes about his sources in *An American Plague: The True and Terrifying Story of the Yellow Fever Epidemic of 1793* provide readers with additional information about the varied perspectives of his sources. Writing about one of his sources, J. Henry Helmuth's *A Short Account of the Yellow Fever in*

Philadelphia: For the Reflecting Christian (1794), Murphy states: "His aim was to convince readers that the fever was a warning from God for the sins of the entire community. One way he attempted to do this was by writing detailed 'you are there' scenes of the devastation." Murphy's notes are as entertaining as they are enlightening, and they help readers understand the context in which the accounts were written.

Many critics of children's nonfiction feel quite strongly about the documentation of sources, and yet there doesn't seem to be any clear consensus as to what level and type of documentation should be used. There is more agreement among adults about *why* information should be documented than *how* authors should do it, and the most common reason given is for the benefit of child readers. As Sandip Wilson points out in her excellent article "Getting Down to the Facts in Children's Nonfiction Literature: A Case for the Importance of Sources," sources go beyond answering the basic question of "How does the author know that?" to showing children the important conventions of nonfiction literature.

Both these roles can be seen in the exemplary notes provided by Scott Reynolds Nelson and Marc Aronson in their book *Ain't Nothing but a Man: My Quest to Find the Real John Henry.* In addition to notes about sources and an annotated bibliography suggesting further readings, Marc Aronson has provided a short essay called "How to Be a Historian" that outlines six steps, using examples from Nelson's John Henry research to illustrate his points. This directly engages young readers in the actual research methodology used by historians, as it tells them something about how Nelson gathered his historical evidence.

While the documentation of sources is clearly an important factor in evaluating nonfiction, the success of a book should not rise or fall based solely on its citations or lack thereof. Of all the factors I have described that make up a nonfiction book, documentation is clearly the easiest to assess: Either it's there or it isn't. For this reason, I suspect that some critics who are willing to write off a book due only to a lack of documentation are opting for the easy way out. They are disregarding some of the more challenging questions: What is the author's authority? How is the material organized? Does the design clarify the sequence of ideas? Do the illustrations extend the text? What sort of writing style does the author use? The answers to all these questions and more ultimately add up to the success or failure of a book of information. We at least owe it to our audience of readers to consider them all as we evaluate nonfiction.

CHAPTER 3

Traditional Literature

Traditional literature is a general term that applies to myths, epics, legends, tall tales, fables, and folktales that originated in oral story-telling and have been passed down from one generation to the next. The original authors of these tales are unknown, although today the stories themselves have sometimes come to be associated with the name of the person who first collected the oral version and wrote it down. Thus, much of the folk literature of Europe, for example, is attributed to the Brothers Grimm, who were among the first scholars to record the tales as ordinary people told them in the early nineteenth century.

The act of collecting oral stories for the purposes of recording them is an academic pursuit. For the past century and a half, it has been a particular preoccupation of anthropologists who wish to pre-serve the stories for scholarly cultural studies. Most of the traditional literature from non-European sources was initially collected for these purposes, not as a potential source of entertainment for American children.

How is it, then, that contemporary American children's literature abounds with traditional literature? There seem to be several factors at work. First, there is a long tradition of myth, legends, and folktales being served up as children's literature. With the European fairy tales, for example, while children were undoubtedly part of the audience for the oral tales in their original context, they were not the sole, or even primary, audience. But once the tales were written down, they gradually came to be seen as the province of children, due to many of the common characteristics they share that make them very appealing and accessible to children: concentrated action; stock characters; patterned language; elements of fantasy; and simple themes, such as good versus evil and the weak overcoming the strong.

A second factor that has encouraged the link between traditional literature and children's books is the emphasis on oral storytelling as a part of library programming for children. Librarians trained as storytellers quite naturally seek out stories from traditional oral sources as likely candidates for their own retellings. This creates a demand for publishing in this area, which in turn makes critics from the children's library field fairly welcoming and receptive to a wide range of traditional material being published as children's books.

Third, with the increasing demand for multicultural literature, there has been a tremendous increase in the amount of traditional literature from non-European sources over the past two decades or so. Critic Lyn Miller-Lachmann attributes this to the fact that folktales offer advantages to those who wish to expand multicultural literature: ready-made characters and plots that can be extracted from sources in the public domain that require no royalty payments. But children's book editor Phoebe Yeh cautions that retelling and illustrating folktales from other cultures raises complex issues of authenticity. She points out that it is naive to assume this is the "safest" way to increase the number of multicultural books. A good example of this fallacy is the multiple "multicultural" variants we've seen over the past two decades of different familiar folktales. In her article "Proceed with Caution: Using Native American Folktales in the Classroom," professor Debbie Reese provides a thorough analysis of a single story that was taken from the Zuni people and recast as a Cinderella story in a picture book retelling. By comparing the picture book text to an authentic Zuni text, she was able to point out details that were added or changed to fit European values and make the story seem closer to "Cinderella" than it actually was.

A final factor that contributes to the abundance of traditional literature in contemporary U.S. publishing for children has to do with the power of the stories themselves. Many of them are exceptionally good stories, plain and simple. Who can *not* identify with the growing vexation of the Baby Bear upon finding his porridge eaten, his chair broken, and an intruder in his bed? Who can *not* be moved by John Henry's valiant but unsuccessful attempt to race a steam drill? Ultimately, the tales have survived for their sheer power as stories dealing with universal human truths.

CLASSIFICATION OF TRADITIONAL LITERATURE

Scholars agree on several different categories of traditional literature, and these definitions can be useful to anyone evaluating traditional literature for children. The first step to take is to determine the category into which the tale falls. This will not only help in your overall approach to the book as you read and critique it but also will allow you to use more precise language when you express your opinions of the book.

Here are the most common categories of traditional literature.

MYTHOLOGY

These stories explain the existence and nature of the world, and generally feature gods and goddesses as their primary characters, although mortals occasionally put in an appearance. Myths are often considered to be sacred stories in their culture of origin.

EPICS

Long, episodic stories of adventure, grounded in mythology but featuring a mortal hero. The best-known epics in the Western tradition are *The Iliad* and *The Odyssey*.

LEGENDS

Stories based on supposedly real people and their heroic deeds and adventures. Part of the intrigue of legends is that their characters, such as King Arthur and Johnny Appleseed, are said to have a historical basis, yet their stories are a mix of fantasy and reality.

TALL TALES

A type of legend in which the hero's exploits are highly exaggerated and retold in a hyperbolic style, generally to the point of being hilariously funny.

URBAN LEGENDS

A recently identified type of contemporary oral tale that recounts bizarre or supernatural occurrences, sworn to be true as the teller generally claims the event happened to a friend of a friend. In spite of their name, they can be set in any real place, urban or rural. These tales are popular with older children, as well as teenagers and adults, and are beginning to make their way into published literature for children.

FABLES

A very short story which teaches a moral or a lesson about conduct. Fables rarely feature more than two characters, and the characters are often animals.

FOLKTALES

Fanciful short stories with either human or animal characters. Most folktales have fast-moving plots in which good is eventually rewarded and evil is punished. Folktales themselves have been divided into several categories.

Cumulative: stories such as "The House That Jack Built" that are structured with the repetition of an ever-increasing accumulation of details.

Pourquoi: stories that explain the origins of natural traits, such as "Why Mosquitoes Buzz in People's Ears."

Beast tales: stories in which animals talk and behave as people.

Fairy tales: Also called "magic tales" or "wonder tales," stories with elements of magic and enchantment. They may include supernatural characters such as witches, wizards, elves, dragons, and even occasionally fairies.

Realistic: The rarest type of folktale, these are stories with human characters and no magic elements.

As you evaluate any book based on traditional literature, one of the first things you should do is to determine the *tale type*. Is the story a retelling of a myth? Is it a legend? Or *pourquoi* tale? Sometimes this information will be given to you in the book's subtitle or in an author's note, but most often you will have to make this judgment yourself by applying what you know about the categories of traditional literature. Among children's literature professionals, the above-named categories are widely known and understood, so your use of these descriptive terms in published reviews will be especially helpful.

Traditional stories from all these categories are published in the United States for children each year, although the majority of these are folktales. Many are published individually, a single story presented in a thirty-two-page picture book; others are published as collections of tales in one volume. Whatever the mode of presentation, there are critical standards that can be applied to all traditional literature when it is being retold for a child audience. These standards relate to the context in which the literature is created: first, as an oral literature that undoubtedly changed as it was passed from storyteller to storyteller; next, as it was consciously collected and recorded for posterity; and finally, as it was taken from one written source, reshaped, retold, and re-created into another as a book for children.

ORIGINAL SOURCES

The evaluation of traditional literature begins with a healthy dose of curiosity about the original source of the material. Ask yourself: Where did this story originate? Because very few writers of children's books have primary contact with the actual source of an oral story, they must generally rely on a printed version that was collected for another purpose by another person.

In recent years there has been a growing demand that authors who retell traditional literature for children cite the printed sources from which they derived the story. In her excellent article "Cite the Source: Reducing Cultural Chaos in Picture Books," the critic and folklore scholar Betsy Hearne has evaluated the methods authors currently use for citing sources in picture book folktales and has found that they fall into five different categories:

1. **Model source notes** cite specific source(s) and provide a description of the cultural context in which the story was told, as well as a description of any changes the author made in his or her retelling.

2. **Well-made source notes** cite the specific source(s) in a highly visible presentation at the beginning or end of the book and may also include cultural details related to the story.

3. **Fine-print source notes** cite specific source(s) in a less visible manner, generally in small print on the copyright page.

4. **Background-as-source notes** give general information about the culture from which the tale comes and sometimes information about the story itself, without citing a specific printed source.

5. **Nonexistent source notes** provide no information on sources at all beyond, perhaps, a subtitle such as "An Old Tale" or "A Navajo Legend."

Dr. Hearne goes on to argue convincingly that as critics we should consider types 4 and 5 completely unacceptable. She writes: "[I]t's time to declare that part of a great picture-book folktale *is* the source note, that context is important to text."

Occasionally, an author will collect a folktale directly from an oral rather than a printed source, and the same standards for source notes apply, perhaps even more stringently. As Dr. Hearne points out: "It is one thing to adapt a folktale from a printed source, which should, of course, be cited. It is another to collect a story from an oral source and not attribute it, which violates basic folklore and storytelling ethics."

Source notes are invaluable to the critic. Beyond assessing the level and quality of the note itself, you may choose to seek out the original printed source to compare it to the book you are evaluating. This is an especially important step to take when the tale is previously unknown to you or when it comes from an unfamiliar culture or tradition. By comparing the adaptation to the original, you can determine the quality of the author's retelling. What details have changed? Is there a logical reason for any changes, omissions, or additions? Has the author successfully re-created the original tone of the story? What elements reflect the author's own style?

Kevin Crossley-Holland's model source notes for the retellings in his book *British Folk Tales: New Versions* offer capsule histories of the tales themselves, so that even tales that are familiar to readers can be read with new eyes. Look, for example, at his source note on the well-loved story "Goldilocks and the Three Bears":

The Doctor by Robert Southey (1837)
The earliest known version of this nursery tale was written down by Eleanor Mure in 1831, but I have chosen to follow the clean lines and formulaic repetitions of Southey's version. Southey, however, described his visitor to the three bears as a "little old Woman" with an "ugly, dirty, head"; I have bowed to more recent taste . . . in changing her into Goldilocks—a form she first took in 1904 (Old Nursery Stories and Rhymes, illustrated by Joan Hassall) after passing several incarnations, including Silver-Hair (1849), Silver-Locks (1858), and Golden Hair (1868). I have also dropped most of Southey's little moral asides. . . .

Crossley-Holland's version of "The Three Bears" includes several details not commonly found in other retellings: The bears are all male and are described as "the great, huge bear"; "the middle bear"; and "the little, small, wee bear" rather than the more familiar Papa Bear, Mama Bear, and Baby Bear. Goldilocks expresses her frustration with the words "Bother and bother!" and "Dash and dash!" When the bears return home, they find evidence of an intruder through clues Goldilocks has left behind: spoons left in porridge bowls, chair cushions left flattened and out of place, pillows and blankets rumpled on the bears' beds. These details have generally been omitted from other retellings, in which the three bears seem to know instinctively that someone's been eating their porridge, sitting in their chairs, and sleeping in their beds. Lastly the Crossley-Holland version ends with one further formulaic repetition: As the bears examine their beds, each of their voices enters into Goldilocks's dreams. The great, huge bear's voice is like thunder rumbling; the middle bear's voice is like " . . . somebody speaking in a dream"; and finally the shrill, high-pitched voice of the little, small, wee bear wakes her up.

A quick consultation with Southey's version, which can be found in Iona and Peter Opie's *The Classic Fairy Tales*, reveals that most of these details came directly from the original source. Goldilocks's interjections were Crossley-Holland's invention, but the description of the bears, the trail of evidence, and the effect of the voices on a sleeping Goldilocks were all part of the 1837 version. By comparing his version to the original, we can see that Crossley-Holland's skill comes through in his deliberate decisions based on thorough research and in his lucid retelling that restores the story's original charm.

Other retellers have strayed a bit further from the source in their retellings of "Goldilocks and the Three Bears" but have come up with equally enchanting versions. Byron Barton's version, *The Three Bears*, takes a minimalist approach by scaling the text down to the least number of words that can be used to tell the story. His concise text is well matched with boldly colored, uncluttered illustrations, making the edition perfect for very young children who are hearing the story for the very first time. James Marshall's text in *Goldilocks and the Three Bears* adds many humorous asides; on noticing a lot of coarse brown fur around the bears' house, for example, Goldilocks surmises, "They must have kitties." The author, too, adds occasional comments himself, in the spirit of Dr. Southey's moral asides. Marshall's tone, combined with his wry illustrations, makes it clear that he is inviting children to laugh at Goldilocks's bad manners and errors in judgment, mistakes they themselves would *never* make. His edition is ideal for children who are already familiar with the story and who are thus likely to enjoy Marshall's unique additions. Margaret Willey strays a bit further from the original by making the three bears' abode more rustic and bearlike in *The 3 Bears and Goldilocks*. When Goldilocks comes upon the crude little cabin that has floors strewn with " . . . leaves and berry stems and pine cones and fish bones and thick, brown fur," she pitches in to tidy the place up, thinking that whoever lives there will appreciate her efforts. But the physical labor makes her hungry and tired, leading her to sample the bowls of porridge and the beds. In this retelling the author provides a bit of invented backstory for children who are familiar with the original story and have been left wondering about Goldilocks's motivation.

NARRATIVE STYLE

The most successful retellings of traditional stories for children maintain something of the flavor of their oral origins. As Betsy Hearne has pointed out, these stories should come alive when they're read out loud: Repetition, rhythm, and robust sound are often important features in oral stories.

Julius Lester is especially gifted as a teller of tales from African-American traditions and is perhaps one of the best writers when it comes to capturing the sound of oral storytelling in written form for children.

Lester achieves this by using short sentences, natural dialogue, humorous exaggeration, surprising metaphors, and by occasionally addressing his audience directly.

> *The next day John Henry went to town. He met up with the meanest man in the state, Ferret-Faced Freddy, sitting on his big white horse. You know what he was doing? He was thinking of mean things to do. Ferret-Faced Freddy was so mean, he cried if he had a nice thought.*
>
> *John Henry said, "Freddy, I'll make you a bet. Let's have a race. You on your horse. Me on my legs. If you and your horse win, you can work me as hard as you want for a whole year. If I win, you have to be nice for a year."*
>
> *Ferret-Faced Freddy laughed an evil laugh. "It's a deal, John Henry." His voice sounded like bat wings on tombstones.*

Julius Lester's narrative is not only easy to read aloud but also easy for listeners to understand and follow, due to his faithfulness to oral traditions.

Margaret Read MacDonald is a professional storyteller whose oral style is reflected in her written retellings of folktales. Like Lester, she uses a lot of short and natural-sounding dialogue. She also uses recurring phrases to give the story a predictable pattern, making it easier for children to listen to and remember. In *Mabela the Clever*, line breaks and boldface and uppercase type are used to add emphasis for anyone reading it aloud.

> *Then Mabela remembered*
> *something else her father*
> *always said. "Mabela, when*

you are out and about, keep
your eyes open and LOOK
AROUND YOU."

Mabela turned her head
just a little to the left,
just a little to the right.
She did NOT see a LONG
line of mice. She saw a
SHORT line of mice and
the CAT VERY CLOSE!

Many storytellers choose to take on a more formal tone in their retellings to reflect the serious nature of the tale they are telling. But even with stories of this kind, the original oral style is generally direct and to the point. Note, for example, the style of the following Lenape tale from John Bierhorst's collection *The White Deer, and Other Stories Told by the Lenape*, recorded directly from an oral source, Lenape elder Nora Thompson Dean:

Well, this is a story about a squirrel. At one time he was a very huge creature, and he went about the lands on the prairies—and the woods.

He killed everything he saw, and he would eat these different animals—the lynx, and the weasels, and wolves, everything he'd catch—he would eat these creatures.

Compare that authentic oral style with the opening sentences Abenaki writer-storyteller Joseph Bruchac uses in a tale of the neighboring Passamaquoddy, "The Girl and the Chenoo":

Long ago, there was a girl whose older brothers were hunters. When they went on their hunting trips far into the forest, she would some-times go with them. Because she was always ready to hear their stories, they called her Little Listener and were happy to have her along. As she was the youngest, Little Listener was usually the one chosen to stay behind and take care of their camp.

While we can see that Bruchac's written narrative is a bit more polished, he still maintains the qualities of an oral tale by quickly establishing the time, setting, and main character of the story and then moving right into the action. Very few words are wasted on physical descriptions or on creating a context for the story. And his tone is respectful without being reverential.

Because all traditional literature has its origins in oral storytelling, it is important to look closely at the language that is used in any tale you evaluate. Does the text read well aloud? What words contribute to the quality Dr. Hearne describes as "robust sound"? Do you notice elements that give the text a flavor of oral storytelling, such as colloquial speech or occasional use of second person or questions? Do you notice a repetition of any catch phrases, such as the Three Bears' observation "Someone has been sitting in my chair"?

The oral origins of the tale will also dictate aspects of plot and character. Since these tales move along quickly, with little time to establish setting and character motivations, we expect rapid transitions and concentrated action. The text itself might seem choppy and dis-jointed if the author doesn't use vivid language or establish patterns through repetition. Consider, for example, how *The Three Bears* might read without its richly patterned language:

Three bears decided to go for a walk while their porridge was cool-ing. While they were gone, a little girl named Goldilocks entered their house. She tasted the porridge in the first two bowls and then ate all the porridge in the third one. She sat in the bears' chairs and broke the smallest one. She went upstairs and tried out all the bears' beds. She found the smallest one to be the most comfortable, and she fell asleep on it. She was still sleeping when the bears returned home. They noticed someone had been eating their porridge and sitting in their chairs. Then they went upstairs and noticed someone had been sleeping in their beds, too. The smallest bear cried out, "She's still here!" That woke Goldilocks up and she jumped out the window and ran away. The three bears never saw her again.

Given this basic bare-bones version, we can see how much the story depends on the use of repetition and pattern in the language that is used to retell it. In trying to determine the quality of a retelling, it can be helpful to think of the story in terms of its most basic plot outline, as I have done above with "The Three Bears." This will make the reteller's language stand out. How has the author used language to make the retelling engaging and easy to listen to? What descriptive phrases and actions are used to characterize the key players in the story? You will note, for example, that the three bears lose all their distinguishing characteristics when they are no longer described in terms of size or their connections to Goldilocks's response to their individual chairs, beds, and bowls of porridge.

ILLUSTRATIONS

At the end of the twentieth century, we saw a tremendous increase in the publication of picture book versions of folktales for children, partly to meet the increasing demands for multicultural literature and partly to meet the increasing demands from artists who use picture books as a means of showcasing their art. It was not unusual, for example, to see more than one picture book version of the same story published in any given year. While there have been fewer picture book folktales published since 2000, they continue to be a mainstay of children's literature.

Because traditional literature is by its nature generally devoid of extensive description, these stories are ripe for countless illustrative treatments by artists with distinctive and diverse styles. Four picture book versions of "Hansel and Gretel" published within a five-year period, for example, contain remarkably similar texts—all were taken from faithful English translations of the story as it appeared in the Brothers Grimm's 1812 *Children's and Household Tales.* But in the hands of four different illustrators, no two versions look alike.

Austrian artist Lisbeth Zwerger emphasizes the isolation and abandonment of Hansel and Gretel by making the two solitary children the focal point of every illustration. Very little attention is given to background details of any kind, and often we see only their two figures set against a backdrop of a somber earth tones that fade into nothingness. Conversely, American artist Susan Jeffers pays great attention to the children's natural surroundings, with leaves, flowers, birds, and other forest creatures in great abundance placed in the foreground of nearly every illustration. Her art suggests that it is human contact, not the forest, that holds danger for the pair.

Another American artist, Paul O. Zelinsky, gives the story a more literal interpretation, with his richly detailed oil paintings that suggest the works of seventeenth-century Dutch genre painters. His attention to clothing styles and household interiors puts the story into a definite historical context. So, too, do the illustrations by British artist Anthony Browne; however, he places the story a little closer to home by setting it in the late twentieth century: Hansel and Gretel's bleak existence, as they sit around a bare kitchen table, includes a blaring television in the background; and, as they lie in bed at night, a bottle of Oil of Olay sits on their stepmother's dresser. Browne's illustrations also add a psychological layer to the story by subtly suggesting that the stepmother and the witch are one and the same.

Personal tastes aside, none of these versions is necessarily superior to the others or a more faithful rendition of the original tale. Each one stands out as distinctive; and happily there is plenty of room for them all. By looking at multiple versions of the same tale, we can even sharpen our evaluative skills, as it leads us to think about those elements that are truly original and to consider how well they complement the story.

Complications arise when an artist attempts to illustrate a story from outside his or her realm of cultural experience. If the artist has little or no background in a particular area and is unwilling or unable to do thorough research, he or she is in danger of misrepresenting the story through illustrations, especially if an attempt is made to imitate "native" styles. It is very difficult for an outsider to extract details effectively without an understanding of the overall context from which they come. That is not to say it can't be done. Ed Young, for example, is known for his attention to authentic detail in the artwork he creates for traditional stories from other cultures. In Kimiko Kajikawa's *Tsunami!*, for example, Young accurately depicts the clothing, hairstyles, and architecture characteristic of mid-nineteenth-century Japan.

Beyond judging the quality of the illustrations themselves, as you would do with any picture book, think about how well they complement the story. Has the artist tried to give a sense of the place and culture from which the tale comes and, if so, has he or she succeeded? Does the style the artist used blend well with the tone of the story? What details has the artist added to expand characterization or define setting? Does the artist add a personal interpretation to the story through the use of mood or symbols?

COLLECTIONS

In addition to picture-book editions of single tales, many traditional stories are published in collections of stories which are generally aimed at children from ages eight to twelve. While these collections may include occasional illustrations, the emphasis here is on the stories themselves, and there is generally some unifying characteristic that binds them together. They may be stories from a particular nation or ethnic group, for example, such as Sheldon Oberman's *Solomon and the Ant, and Other Jewish Folktales*, or they may be stories of a particular type, as in Jane Yolen's collection of folktales from around the world with strong female protagonists, *Not One Damsel in Distress*.

DOCUMENTATION OF SOURCES

Even when stories come from a common cultural source, the reteller generally consults a variety of original source material to pull together a collection of stories. Because this is most often the case, we expect the author to provide documentation and source notes for each story included in the collection.

Author Alvin Schwartz sets the standard for this sort of documentation in his collections of folklore aimed at children. Even in his simplest books, such as the beginning reader *In a Dark, Dark Room, and Other Scary Stories*, he includes source notes titled "Where the Stories Come From" that are aimed at the beginning readers themselves. His popular collections of frightening folklore for older children include extensive notes; for the twenty-nine stories included in *Scary Stories to Tell in the Dark*, for example, Schwartz provides what Betsy Hearne has referred to as "model source notes." To research and document the stories he retold, he consulted eighty-four print sources and more than a dozen informants (both children and adults who shared their scary stories with him). In his notes he acknowledges the sources he used, discusses variants, and tells how he arrived at the final version that appears in his book.

ORGANIZATION

Schwartz also organizes the stories into sections by type: jump stories, ghost stories, scary things, urban legends, and humorous stories. Each section is introduced with a one- or two-sentence description of the story type, and at the end of the book more extensive notes give further background about each of the tale types, including such things as various techniques for telling a jump tale and the current social environment that makes urban legends appealing.

Other compilers have chosen to organize collections by places or cultures of origin, or by subject. When you evaluate a collection of traditional tales, think about how it is organized. Will the organization assist readers who may be looking for just one or two particular tales? Will it invite readers to approach the collected stories as one continuous narrative? Does the author provide a written introduction to the stories in each section that explains how the part is distinctive and how it relates to the collection as a whole? What is the range of tale types within each section, as well as the range of tales in the entire book?

LITERARY FOLKTALES

These tales are not part of traditional literature, but I will mention them here because they are often confused with traditional tales. Rather than originating within a particular culture's oral storytelling tradition, a literary folktale is written by a known author who uses the characteristics we associate with folktales: concentrated action, stock characters, elements of fantasy, and simple themes. Hans Christian Andersen and Oscar Wilde are perhaps the best-known authors of this type of tale; however, many contemporary authors try their hands at this as well. They are often difficult to distinguish from true folktales, so be on the lookout for descriptive phrases, such as "an original tale," in subtitles or flap copy. Also, check the CIP on the copyright page. The Library of Congress assigns the Dewey decimal number 398 to traditional literature, 290 to mythology, and [FIC] or [E] to literary folktales, although it is not always infallible in its classifications.

FRACTURED FAIRY TALES

Somewhere between true folktales and literary folktales fall *fractured fairy tales*, playful variants on familiar stories and characters. Many scholars cite James Thurber as the first American writer to fracture a tale, with "The Little Girl and the Wolf," a send-up of "Little Red Riding Hood" that was published in *The New Yorker* in 1939. The term "fractured fairy tale" itself comes from a regular segment that was part of the *Rocky and Bullwinkle* cartoon series that ran from 1959 to 1964. Julie Cummins defines it as "A classic folk or fairy tale rewritten with tongue-in-cheek humor or as a spoof using twists and spins on the story's features; text and visual references poke fun at the original, resulting in a witty, clever, and entertaining tale."

In children's literature, Jon Scieszka and Lane Smith have set the standard for fractured fairy tales, beginning with their popular recasting of "The Three Little Pigs," *The True Story of the 3 Little Pigs* by A. Wolf. They turn the original on its head by telling the story from the wolf's point of view. He was merely trying to borrow a cup of sugar from his porcine neighbors so he could bake a cake for his grandmother. Was it his fault that their houses were so poorly constructed that they fell down when he sneezed? Smith's illustrations add to the humor by consistently contradicting the wolf's claims of his innocence. David Wiesner uses illustration to twist the same story in a completely different direction in *The Three Pigs* by inviting us to look beyond the borders of the page itself. In his fractured tale, the wolf huffs and puffs and blows the pigs right out of the story. Outside the tale, they become realistic, three-dimensional pigs who look right at the reader before they wander through other traditional tales, taking on the characteristics of the various art styles represented in each one.

"The Three Little Pigs" seems to be a favorite target for fracturing, but any familiar tale can find new life when an author and artist play with setting, characters, point of view, or a reversal of standard elements. For fractured fairy tales to be completely successful with children, they must begin with traditional tales that children know well. Otherwise, the humor will probably fall flat. Happily, authors have a wealth of traditional tales from which to choose.

CHAPTER 4

Poetry, Verse, Rhymes, and Songs

Rhythm, rhyme, and the pleasurable sounds that words make can appeal to children from a very early age. It is no accident that lullabies are sung to soothe babies and nursery rhymes are recited to entertain them. Children of all ages like the sounds of poetry in language. Older children chant rhymes as they play games and jump rope. They revise the lyrics of commercial jingles to amuse their peers and twist names and words to taunt their enemies. They re-create the rhythms and rhymes of popular music to pass the time as they wait for the school bus in the morning. We find an appetite for poetry everywhere we find children.

Yet many children claim to dislike poetry. In all likelihood what they dislike is the *study* of poetry. Because poetry is defined in part by form and structure, over the years, children in school have been forced to think about poems in these terms. Many adults themselves have unpleasant memories of being forced to dissect a poem to analyze its meaning, and they have come to associate this unpleasantness with poetry in general. But poetry need not be picked apart to be understood and appreciated. Poems speak to children through sound, images, and ideas.

THE SOUND OF POETRY

Poetry uses words in musical, rhythmic patterns that delight small children, even before they understand the meaning of the words. As children get older, they are better able to appreciate the subtleties of poetic form and content, but young children seem to be especially attracted to the regular structured patterns, more aptly called *verse*.

Rhyme, the repetition of the same or similar sounds, is an important part of verse and, to some extent, poetry. There are many kinds of rhyme, but when most people use the word, they are generally referring to *end rhyme* only. End rhyme is the regularly occurring echo that is used in a uniform pattern at the conclusion of lines, and it is the hallmark of conventional verse, particularly verse that is aimed at very young children. While it can be pleasing to the ear and may make a poem easier to listen to and remember, it can also lead to a sing-song regularity that deadens the senses. In fact, many believe that end rhyme is such an artificial and unnatural way of using language, in the hands of a lesser poet, it can destroy the essence of poetry. Writers can easily become so bound to rhyme that it dictates the word choice, and the words lose their power and meaning. That is the opposite of what a poet strives for.

Many other devices of sound contribute to rhyme in a pleasurable but less obvious way. These include *alliteration* (the repetition of initial consonant sounds), *assonance* (the repetition of vowel sounds), and *consonance* (the repetition of final consonants). Karla Kuskin uses all the above sound devices in her poem "Thistles."

Thirty thirsty thistles
Thicketed and green
Growing in a grassy swamp

Purple-topped and lean
Prickly and thistly
Topped by tufts of thorns
Green mean little leaves on them
And tiny purple horns
Briary and brambly
A spiky, spiney bunch of them.
A troop of bright-red birds came by
And had a lovely lunch of them.

Both poetry and verse have some sort of rhythm, called *meter*. The lengths of a poem's lines and the pattern of stressed and unstressed syllables constitute its meter. It not only contributes to the way a poem sounds but also can reinforce the poem's meaning. Meter can be used to slow the reader down and give us a sense of quiet contemplation or dreaming, or to move us along quickly to communicate such things as playful movement. Note how the poet Eloise Greenfield uses short lines to reinforce meaning in this stanza from her poem about a child in motion:

When Lessie runs she runs so fast that
Sometimes she falls down
But she gets right up and brushes her knees
And runs again as fast as she can
Past red houses
    and parked cars
    and bicycles
    and sleeping dogs
    and cartwheeling girls

> *and wrestling boys*
> *and Mr. Taylor's record store*
> *All the way to the corner*
> *To meet her mama*

The two- and three-word lines list the people and things Lessie passes as she's running, and also give a sense of her feet pounding on the pavement in her breathless sprint down the street, until she finally slows down when she reaches the corner.

Contrast this with the effect that meter has in Douglas Florian's poem about waiting for winter to end.

> *When winter winds wind down and end . . .*
> *Then spring is coming round the bend.*
>
> *When winter ice begins to thaw . . .*
> *Then spring is knocking at the door.*
>
> *When winter snow is nowhere found . . .*
> *Then spring, you know, has come to town.*

Florian has cleverly used meter to slow down the reading of the first line of each stanza and to speed up the reading of the second, giving us a sense of winter's prolonged stay and the spring's welcome arrival.

Modern poetry had gradually moved away from a reliance on a strict rhythm and the use of end rhymes. Poems need not rhyme at all, and *free verse* breaks away from formal metrical patterns altogether. Arnold Adoff is one of the best-known children's poets who brings a modern vision to poetry. His poems often tell a story by combining strong feeling with action.

> *i am near the shoulder*
> > *of the girl*
> > *in the lead*
>
> *and maybe this lead girl*
> > > *looks*
> > > > *back*
> *for a second*
> *to see if i am still*
> > *on her shoulder*
>
> *then my eyes*
> *tell her*
> > *good*
> > > *bye*

In Adoff's poems, the placement of the words on the page is almost like a road map, giving readers guidance as to how they should read the poems aloud.

THE IMAGES OF POETRY

Since poems are compact, there can be no wasted words. The poet carefully chooses precise, exact words to evoke the desired mood or feeling, or to surprise the reader with an unexpected—but perfect—comparison. Poetry uses *metaphor*, bringing unrelated things together to point out similarities or differences. Pay close attention to the way Gwendolyn

Brooks uses words to create images and feelings in "Cynthia in the Snow" from her book *Bronzeville Boys and Girls*:

It SUSHES.
It hushes
The loudness in the road.
It flitter-twitters,
And laughs away from me.
It laughs a lovely whiteness,
And whitely whirs away,
To be
Some otherwhere,
Still white as milk or shirts.
So beautiful it hurts.

Brooks uses imagery to appeal to the senses of hearing, sight, and touch, making us feel as though we are right in the midst of a snow flurry. Her playful use of words—"laughs away from me," "whitely," and "otherwhere"—is original and inventive and yet can be immediately understood. On a metaphorical level, Brooks writes about snow as if it were a person, another child perhaps, teasing and enticing Cynthia as a playmate might do.

THE IDEAS OF POETRY

Like "Cynthia in the Snow," good children's poetry gives fresh vision to common things and experiences. It can appeal to the intellect as well as the emotions, as it extends and enriches meaning in everyday life. In looking at children's poetry on an intellectual level, we need to keep in mind the typical interests and concerns of childhood: relationships with friends and family, the outdoors, daily routines, play, animals, and

73

ordinary everyday things such as safety pins or socks—these are pieces of the child's world. We can find them all in good poetry for children.

When we evaluate children's poetry, we need to consider the quality of the poetry itself by thinking about how it sounds, what it says, and how it says it. Read poetry aloud. A good poem sounds natural, even if it rhymes. Look at the words that have been used to compose the poem. Do they seem unchangeable? What kinds of specific and implied comparisons has the poet made? How has imagery been used? Think about the idea presented in the poem. Does it show a fresh view of something with which a child is likely to be familiar? Does it appeal to the mind through the senses? Does it leave a lingering image in the mind of the reader?

In addition to thinking about the quality of the poetry itself, we also need to consider the manner in which it is presented in a book. Poetry published for children exists in great quantity and variety. We find books that appeal to all ages from infancy up through the teen years. There are anthologies of classic poems, some of which were written specifically for children and some of which were written for adults but can be enjoyed by children. There are collections of poems by individual poets. There are single poems that are illustrated and published as individual picture books, as well as picture-book texts written in verse. And there are collections of songs published in anthologies, in addition to single songs published in picture-book editions. There are novels written in verse. Because poetry, rhymes, and verse appeal to a broad range of ages, we need to think in terms of audience when we evaluate individual volumes of poetry. Let's take a look at some of these categories, beginning with rhymes for the very youngest.

NURSERY RHYMES
Nursery rhymes recited to children and handed down through generations have come to be associated with the appropriately fanciful name

Mother Goose. In their authoritative work on the subject, *The Oxford Dictionary of Nursery Rhymes*, folklore scholars Peter and Iona Opie remark that while many scholarly studies have attempted to analyze the symbolic and historical nature of the rhymes, these interpretations are largely speculative. The rhymes themselves have survived not because of a great underlying meaning—indeed, many of them make little sense at all—but because of their sound: "[T]hese trivial verses have endured where newer and more ambitious compositions have become dated and forgotten. They have endured often for nine or ten generations, sometimes for considerably more, and scarcely altered in their journey."

While surviving as oral literature for generations, the rhymes began to be published in books especially created for children in the early eighteenth century. They are among the earliest children's books published in both England and the United States. For the most part the rhymes they contain are familiar to English-speaking children today: "Baa, Baa, Black Sheep," "Little Jack Horner," and "This Little Pig Went to Market" among them.

The rhymes themselves don't change, but the illustrations do. Each year new editions of Mother Goose nursery rhymes are added to the selection of contemporary children's books. Illustrations offer new interpretations or fresh presentations of familiar characters. In his collection *Three Little Kittens, and Other Favorite Nursery Rhymes*, Tony Ross uses a cartoon style to bring out the playful nonsense inherent in most of the rhymes. He also makes visual asides at some of the more perplexing or archaic references; for example, when Jack (of "Jack and Jill" fame) winds up in bed "to mend his head / with vinegar and brown paper," Ross shows him with a huge wad of brown paper stuck loosely atop his head, staring blankly at a bottle of vinegar he's holding in his hand. Ruth Sanderson takes the opposite tack in *Mother Goose and Friends*. Her realistic oil paintings offer a more literal interpretation of the rhymes, showing characters from a past time. She adds a sense of whimsy by including elves and fairies in some of the illustrations. Nina Crews takes a completely different approach with *The Neighborhood Mother Goose*. Forty-one traditional rhymes are illustrated with photographs of contemporary city children that offer a new multicultural dimension to the age-old verses.

How do we evaluate these collections? Look at the illustrations to determine what they add to the rhymes. What scenes did the illustrator choose to show? Due to the harsh and violent nature of many of the rhymes, literal interpretations will not always work. We may enjoy the image of the baby rocking in his cradle on a treetop, but few parents will want to share a picture that shows his unfortunate descent when the bough breaks. Conversely, everyone wants to see Jack and Jill falling down the hill and Humpty Dumpty falling off the wall. A skilled and thoughtful illustrator takes the sensibilities of small children and their parents into consideration.

Look at the selection of rhymes included in the collection. Which rhymes have been included? Is it a fairly comprehensive collection, or is it selective? Are most of the rhymes familiar ones, such as "Little Miss Muffet" and "Little Boy Blue"? Adults who are looking for collections of nursery rhymes to share with their children generally want to find the ones they remember from their childhoods. Less familiar rhymes may be included, but they shouldn't outnumber the common rhymes, unless that is the point of the book, as it is in the Opies' *Tail Feathers from Mother Goose*, a collection of previously unpublished nursery rhymes from various sources housed in the Opie archive. How does the author provide access to the rhymes? Is there an index of titles or of first lines (generally one and the same in nursery rhymes)? If someone were looking for the complete version of "London Bridge Is Falling Down," for example, could it be easily found in the collection?

Since most nursery rhymes are short, they don't all lend themselves to single-rhyme editions of picture books. However, some do. James Marshall has given us a hilarious interpretation in *Old Mother Hubbard and Her Wonderful Dog* by exaggerating the absurdities in the rhyme itself. Bruce McMillan gave us a completely new vision in *Mary Had a Little Lamb* by illustrating it with photographs of an African-American girl wearing glasses and yellow overalls. Tracey Campbell Pearson has created an engaging series of board books featuring individual rhymes such as "Little Miss Muffet," "Diddle, Diddle, Dumpling," and "Little Bo-Peep" that cast contemporary toddlers in the lead roles. In *Little Bo-Peep*, for example, the title character is shown as a baby dropping her stuffed-toy lambs over the side of her crib, only to have them retrieved by her parents when she starts crying. In this case, the brevity of the rhymes have made them perfect choices for board book texts.

HUMOROUS POETRY AND LIGHT VERSE

Nursery rhymes adhere to strict patterns of rhythm and rhyme and would be technically classified as *verse* rather than as poetry. Although the terms "poetry" and "verse" are often used interchangeably, it is fairly easy to draw distinctions between the two, and it's helpful to do so in order to speak and write more precisely. Both poetry and verse use patterned language to condense thoughts and ideas into a structured form. Verse, however, rarely strays from its regular structure; poetry often does. Verse generally deals in lighter subjects and presents ideas as an open-and-shut case, but poetry opens a window onto a thought or experience through the use of metaphor and imagery.

When verse uses trite ideas and hackneyed language, it becomes *doggerel*, an inferior form best reserved for greeting cards. Verse succeeds on a grand scale, however, when it draws humor from wild incongruity or plants verbal surprises within a rigid structure. The *nonsense verse* of nineteenth-century writers Edward Lear and Lewis Carroll continues to delight today's children with its daft impossibilities. There is something about outrageous absurdity bound up in a tight, predictable structure that elementary school-age children find fall-down-on-the-floor funny. Shel Silverstein is a master at this kind of writing, and his collections *Where the Sidewalk Ends*, *A Light in the Attic*, and *Falling Up* are among the best-selling children's hardcover trade books of all time. The zany nonsense verses of Ogden Nash, John Ciardi, and Jack Prelutsky are also extremely popular with children.

Humor in general holds great appeal, from the classic nonsense of Edward Lear to the more subtle uses of humor we see in light verse and poetry. It can open a door into poetry for children and draw them into a vision that offers new insight and meaning. Note, for example, how X. J. Kennedy uses humor to give children a fresh perspective on an ordinary object in his poem "Lighting a Fire":

> *One quick scratch*
> *Of a kitchen match*
> *And giant flames unzip!*
>
> *How do they store*
> *So huge a roar*
> *In such a tiny tip?*

Many writers of children's poetry excel at using wit and humor to stir children's interest and imaginations. Rather than telling children what is funny, these poets are able to see the humor and incongruities in life that children themselves may notice and wonder about. Other than poets and children, for instance, how may people stop to reflect on what happens when you strike a match?

Nonsense verse and humorous poetry differ, to some extent, in form and content, but both offer the reader surprises that inspire laughter. In verse, these surprises are generally dependent on the tension between words and structure. Poetry uses this but also adds an intangible element in the metaphorical tension of ideas that lie under the surface of the poem. X. J. Kennedy does not explicitly compare a kitchen match to a lion, for example, but he suggests it with his choice of the word "roar." As you evaluate humorous verse and poetry, think about the sources of its humor. Does it come from the description of things, people, and places engaged in absurd actions? Or does it come from a more subtle juxtaposition of unlike things or ideas? How does the structure enhance its surprising and pleasurable aspects? Would you look forward to reading the poems aloud to children? Above all, poems are meant to be read aloud—that's often the best test of a poem.

POETRY COLLECTIONS

SINGLE POETS

Children's poems are generally published in collections that may contain anywhere from a dozen to a hundred or more poems. Collections of poems by a single children's poet are quite common, in which case authorship alone may be the one unifying factor. Some poets issue volumes of poetry on a common theme. Douglas Florian, for example, has published separate volumes of poetry on subjects such as winter, dinosaurs, astronomy, and humor. Others issue volumes limited to a certain form. Valerie Worth is known for her collections of very short poems about small things, and Stephen Schnur is known for his acrostic poems about the seasons, such as *Winter: An Alphabet Acrostic*. Haiku is an especially popular form for children's poets; and there have been many volumes that use this form, including Jack Prelutsky's *If Not for the Cat: Haiku* and Michael J. Rosen's *The Cuckoo's Haiku*. Linda Sue Park introduced

American children to *sijo*, a traditional form of Korean poetry that also uses just three lines, in *Tap Dancing on the Roof: Sijo (Poems)*.

ANTHOLOGIES

Anthologies contain the works of many poets. There is an art to collecting and anthologizing poetry that calls for a closer look on the part of the critic. Skillful anthologists pull together poems on a common theme or topic and organize them in an arrangement that makes them aesthetically and intellectually satisfying.

Paul B. Janeczko describes how he sees his work as an anthologist:

> *Poems must connect with other poems. Some associations are obvious, but I look for connections that may not be apparent at first reading. I want my readers to think about why poems are where they are in my collections. I try to bring order to the arrangement of the poems in a way that will give a timid, inexperienced reader of poetry a gentle nudge in a helpful direction.*

We can see how this careful attention to organization is played out in Janeczko's *A Foot in the Mouth: Poems to Speak, Sing, and Shout* just by looking at the table of contents:

Poems for One Voice
Tongue Twisters
Poems for Two Voices
List Poems
Poems for Three Voices
Short Stuff
Bilingual Poems

Rhymed Poems
Limericks
Poems for a Group

Note that in the first six sections, Janeczko alternates simple and more challenging forms to encourage children with different skills. Within each section, there is also a logical arrangement of the poems themselves; and there are even links from section to section. For example, the "Rhymed Poems" section ends with a poem that begins "'What's your name?' / 'Mary Jane' / 'Where do you live?' / 'Womber Lane'" and the subsequent "Limericks" section opens with the classic form "There was a young woman from . . ." There is an overall logical progression, as well: The volume opens with three poems that stress individual identity and, as the chorus of voices grows, ends with Walt Whitman's "I Hear America Singing."

Lee Bennett Hopkins, Nancy Larrick, Michael Rosen, and Jane Yolen are outstanding anthologists of poetry for young readers. Their topical anthologies cover subjects such as animals, family and friends, holidays, science, nature, city life, and bedtime. Both Hopkins and Yolen have compiled collections aimed at particular age groups as well. For *Here's a Little Poem*, Yolen and coauthor Andrew Fusek Peters selected sixty-one outstanding poems for very young children, arranged into four sections: Me, Myself and I; Who Lives in My House?; I Go Outside; and Time for Bed. Lee Bennett Hopkins excels at creating easy-to-read anthologies for young children on subjects such as pets, school, holidays, and sports. His anthologies include well-known children's poets as well as some adult poets whose work is surprisingly easy to read.

There are numerous anthologies of poetry collected for older children along similar lines. One of the most remarkable skills of anthologists for this age level, however, is an ability to read works originally published for adults and select those poems that will speak to the young as well. This skill combines a thorough knowledge of poetry with a thorough knowledge of children and young teenagers. Ruth Gordon, Paul Janeczko, and Naomi Shihab Nye compile stunning anthologies based on poetry from a wide range of times, places, and experiences. These anthologies not only provide young readers with collections of fine poetry but also give them a sense of being connected as individuals to universal human emotions.

Look at the range of poems and poets included in any anthology. Are there new poems as well as older ones? Are the poems selected from a broad range of cultures? Do the poems have a common theme or subject? How are they arranged? Is there an index of titles and/or of first lines?

In the best anthologies the compiler's enthusiasm for poetry is apparent through the careful selections and arrangements he or she has made.

VERSE NOVELS

It is not always easy to categorize books that use poetic forms as their narrative structure. In the past decade, we have seen the rise of *verse novels*, that is, full-length fiction written as a series of connected poems, generally free verse. Virginia Euwer Wolff is often credited as a pioneer in this area with the publication of her novel *Make Lemonade*, although Wolff herself refers to her own writing as "prose in funny-shaped lines." That may be an apt description of many verse novels, but others fall clearly in the realm of poetry.

Sharon Creech's *Love That Dog* and its sequel, *Hate That Cat*, are both written in the voice of young Jack, a boy who claims to hate poetry but eventually finds his poetic voice, thanks to inspiration from a poem by Walter Dean Myers. Throughout both books, Creech plays with poetic forms, as Jack attempts to imitate poems by William Blake, Robert Frost, William Carlos Williams, and, of course, Walter Dean Myers.

Helen Frost is perhaps the most ambitious and the most outstanding author of verse novels for children. Each of her books uses a different type of poetic structure. In *Spinning Through the Universe*, for example, she uses a different poetic form—terza rima, haiku, sonnet, quatern, etc.—to represent each character's voice in Part 1. Part 2 is comprised of acrostic poems in which the acrostic is made up of one line taken from all the previous poems. Frost uses concrete poetry in *Diamond Willow*; each poem has a diamond shape. Both Creech and Frost use poetry to illuminate and reinforce the themes in their books.

SONGS

One might argue that songs were meant to be sung, not written down; but as long as human memories remain fallible, there will be songs committed to the pages of books. As they appear in trade books, songs share many features in common with poetry; unlike most poetry, however, they appeared at first in some form other than writing.

Songbooks for children typically include musical notation as an accompaniment to the text. If the lyrics to a single song are written out in story form as the text of a picture book, the musical notation may appear at the end of the book. The quality of the notation should be evaluated as carefully as text and illustrations. Is the arrangement simple enough to be accessible to children? Is it in a singable key? Is the notation legible and easy to read? Does it include all the song's verses? Have the verses been conveniently placed so that it is possible to follow along if one is playing or singing the song aloud?

John Langstaff is noted for his compilations of British and American folk songs and ballads, such as *Hi! Ho! The Rattlin' Bog, and Other Folk Songs for Group Singing*. The lyrics to each of these songs, drawn from many sources, are accompanied by their musical notation, as well as a brief note that places the song in a historical context. Tish Hinojosa uses a similar approach in her bilingual songbook *Cada Niño/Every Child*, offering historical background for traditional songs and a personal story for the songs she wrote herself.

Other books of song are highly visual. Ashley Bryan is known for the captivating paintings he creates to interpret songs in his books, such as *Let It Shine: Three Favorite Spirituals*. Picture-book editions of single songs are less common but not unknown. Laura Vaccaro Seeger's playful visual interpretation of a traditional folk song, *I Had a Rooster*, uses heavy-stock spiral-bound pages of progressively decreasing size to build the cumulative lines of the song on the left-hand side of the page. The volume also includes a CD of Pete Seeger singing the song so that children can listen to the music as they turn the pages.

A critical approach to books of song requires consideration of some of the standards we use in evaluating poetry as we look at the presentation of language in a structured pattern. It also requires the sort of critical attention we give to folklore, as we must think about source notes, organization, and, in some cases, retelling. Overall we need to ask whether or not one art form (music) has made a successful transition to another (art and literature).

CHAPTER 5

Picture Books

Books for young children combine words with illustrations to tell a story. They are meant to be read aloud while children view the illustrations. Picture books present a special challenge to the critic because they require evaluation of art, text, and how the two work together to create a unique art form. In evaluating picture books, it is also useful for the critic to have an understanding of common interests and cognitive abilities of young children at different stages in their development.

Picture books as we know them today are a fairly recent invention. Children's books that combined short text and illustrations to tell a story were developed by European artists and printers in the mid-nineteenth century; however, it was not until 1928 that the modern American picture book was born with the publication of Wanda Gág's *Millions of Cats*. While earlier efforts set story and pictures side by side, Gág was the first to take art beyond conventional illustration: Her pictures helped to tell the story by using negative space to indicate the passage of time; she varied page layouts, and some illustrations broke out of their frames to extend across two pages. These innovations were immediately imitated and refined by other artists creating books for young children, and very soon they were considered conventions of the art itself.

In 1938, ten years after the publication of *Millions of Cats*, the Caldecott Medal was established to recognize excellence in picture book art. The decades that followed are often thought of as a golden age of American picture books, as this new art form attracted the talents of many gifted artists working in the variety of styles that have flourished in twentieth-century art.

During these years, books with color illustrations often required the artist to go through the painstaking process of separating colors by hand for offset printing. An artist was allowed to work with one, two, three, or four colors, depending on the publisher's budget (the more colors, the more expensive the printing). In three-color art, for instance, an artist might choose to use black, blue, and yellow and would then separate the art by preparing the portions of the picture that were black (generally referred to as a *keyplate*), then painting on separate sheets, called *overlays*, the portions that were blue and the portions that were yellow, so that the finished art would actually be the three sheets, layered one on top of another. This technique required commitment, skill, and patience on the part of the artist, in addition to a thorough understanding of color and an ability to visualize the whole by analyzing its parts. What proportions of blue and yellow, for example, would create the exact shade of green needed? In spite of such constraints (or perhaps because of them), we saw many creative approaches to illustration in black and white or with one or two colors due to the efforts of artists who put their hearts and souls into children's book art.

Changes in technology in the mid-1980s, however, had an enormous impact on book production, especially in the area of picture books. Advances such as high-speed presses, computer technology, and scanning devices not only allowed for accurate reproduction of full-color art but also accomplished it at a lower cost. These changes encouraged the entry of many new fine artists into the field, who employed a great variety of techniques and styles. Children's book art expert Dilys Evans has characterized this as a visual renaissance in which "full-color printing has reached a new plateau of high performance." Even the slightest, most pedestrian story is given the level of art production that was formerly reserved for established and highly acclaimed book creators such as Ludwig Bemelmans, Maurice Sendak, and Marcia Brown.

In the midst of this ever-changing world of picture books, perhaps the factor that remains most constant is the children themselves. Young children may enjoy being dazzled by the latest bold venture in picture book art, but at the same time they may ask to return again and again to the familiar comforts of *Goodnight Moon*. Just what is it about this book that has ensured its success for more than sixty years? It scores high marks in all the areas that matter when it comes to picture books: outstanding text, excellent illustrations, and successful integration of the two. In addition, it holds enormous appeal for young children whose obvious pleasure is then transferred to adults who share the book with them. But, of course, the child's chance at experiencing any picture book as a whole is completely dependent on someone who is willing and able to read the text aloud. Because picture books function best as a shared experience between a fluent reader and a prereader—generally an adult and a young child—in order for a picture book to find true success, it must be good enough to spark this symbiotic relationship.

While all these factors work together to create an aesthetic whole, the critic must break the picture book down into its individual parts in order to evaluate how its components fit together. In this chapter we will look at the picture book in terms of words, pictures, and how the two work together.

TEXT

Anyone who has ever read picture books aloud to children knows just how important the words are. Since most picture books are thirty-two pages in length, and since most of those pages are covered with illustrations, their texts are necessarily short. There is another reason for the economical use of words: Preschoolers simply have limits as to what they can and will take in. Lengthy descriptions and sophisticated abstractions are unnecessary and pointless. In picture books, as in poetry, every word counts. But beyond telling a compelling story in few words, a good picture book text has a distinctive *structure* based on familiar patterns. In order to evaluate picture books, we must ask ourselves not only "What is this story about?" but also "How is this story told?" And when it comes to studying the structural elements of a successful picture book text, we can find no better model than the laureate of the nursery, Margaret Wise Brown.

STRUCTURE

Not too long after Wanda Gág launched American picture books with the publication of *Million of Cats*, writer Margaret Wise Brown entered the scene. As a teacher of two- to five-year-olds in the Bank Street Experimental School during the mid-1930s, Brown was a keen observer of the developmental behavior of her young charges. She was also greatly influenced by the groundbreaking work of her mentor, Lucy Sprague Mitchell, who asserted that, when it came to words, rhythm and sound quality were more important to young children than meaning. It was during this time that Brown began to write her picture books.

Rhythm and sound are the hallmarks of Brown's picture-book texts. She accomplishes this by building a pattern with words that are rooted in a young child's experience and understanding of the world. In Brown's Noisy Books, for example, routines in the everyday world are made extraordinary as children are asked to consider them from the perspective of a little dog named Muffin who experiences the world by hearing it:

> *And then there was a rattle of dishes. That*
> *meant lunch.*
> *What kind of noise did lunch make?*
> *They had celery for lunch.*
> *Could Muffin hear that?*
> *And soup.*
> *Could Muffin hear that?*
> *And raw carrots*
> *and steak*
> *and spinach.*
> *Could Muffin hear that?*
> *And some very quiet custard for dessert.*

All the elements of patterned language that contribute to the success of picture book texts for young children can be found in the above-quoted passage from *The Indoor Noisy Book*. They are rhythm, rhyme, repetition, and questions.

RHYTHM

Note the variation in line lengths, which, as in poetry, gives the reader clues as to how to read the words. But even if these lines were written in paragraphs, they would still maintain most of their rhythm due to Brown's choice of words; "rattle of dishes" sounds very much like what it describes, and the succession of the three trochees, "very quiet custard," naturally causes readers to slow down and speak in softer tones. The line "That meant lunch" packs a punch with its three accented beats that grab and hold the listener's attention. It has the same familiar rhythm as the parental attention grabber: "I said no." Because young children are often inexperienced listeners, their attention wanders easily. Brown places this sort of rhythmic hook at regular intervals to draw them back.

RHYME

While rhyme in *The Indoor Noisy Book* is not obvious, as it is in many other picture books, it is in fact there in the pleasing repetition of sounds and sentences that appear throughout the story. In addition to making a text easier for children to listen to, rhyme also enhances the predictability of a story. When young children listen to a rhyming story, they can generally supply the last word in a couplet or a quatrain, provided the subject is within the realm of their experience.

REPETITION

Brown skillfully alternates repeated lines with the introduction of words or concepts that may be new to children. By doing so she is using a familiar, expected pattern to make children feel comfortable and ready to face the unfamiliar and unexpected. Once she has set up the pattern with, for example, "Could Muffin hear that?" as soon as children hear the words "raw carrots and steak and spinach," they begin to think about the sounds each of these foods makes. And once they have entered this realm of creative thinking, they are more than ready to face the imaginative challenge of "very quiet custard."

The question-answer mode is a language pattern very familiar to young children. The Noisy Books are filled with questions that inspire children to think about what sorts of sounds Muffin is hearing and the sources of various sounds he hears. In the context of picture-book texts, questions serve a couple of different purposes. Since questions are generally read with a different intonation, they add variety to the sound and rhythm of the text. They can also serve as hooks that will pull in wandering minds and help to keep the audience's attention focused. In addition, they directly involve the child in the story, something that not only makes a story more interesting for everyone but also enhances the self-concept of the child. With young children, there is no such thing as a rhetorical question: If the text asks a question, you will probably get answers. The answers to some questions may be obvious to some children: "Is this red?" "Noooo! It's blue!" Others, such as "What kind of noise did lunch make?" require creative thinking and may lead to several possible answers. Lastly, questions help the adult reader silently assess the level of understanding and appreciation on the part of the child audience.

The pleasing sound of patterned language is especially effective in picture books aimed at two- and three-year-olds. It functions almost like a net to catch and hold the young listeners' attention. It should not, however, overwhelm the story. The most successful uses of patterned language reveal themselves when the text is read aloud. Even when preschoolers become more experienced listeners and are able to rely more on meaning, elements of patterned language can greatly enrich stories aimed at three- and four-year-olds, since children at this age level generally enjoy wordplay a great deal.

As children gain experience listening to stories, they begin to develop an understanding that stories follow a regular sequence. This idea can be reinforced by repeated readings of the same story (generally at the child's request), as children become so familiar with the story that they can easily predict what will happen next. Sometimes writers of picture books build predictability into the text with repeated actions or phrases or by using the same sentence structure over and over again. Like patterned language, predictable structures make stories easier for children to listen to and comprehend. They also allow authors to introduce more surprising or unusual elements successfully within a carefully constructed familiar context. The contrast between the predictable and the surprising elements often delights adults as well as children.

In the classic picture book *The Runaway Bunny*, Margaret Wise Brown used predictability in two ways: action and sentence structure. In this story of a small bunny trying to establish a separate identity from his mother while at the same time testing her unconditional love, each action on the bunny's part elicits a predictable reaction on the mother's part:

> *"If you run after me," said the little bunny,*
> *"I will become a fish in a trout stream*
> *and I will swim away from you."*

> *"If you become a fish in a trout stream," said his mother,*
> *"I will become a fisherman and I will fish for you."*

> *"If you become a fisherman," said the little bunny,*
> *"I will become a rock on the mountain, high above you."*

"If you become a rock on the mountain high above me,"
said his mother, "I will be a mountain climber,
and I will climb to where you are."

Children hearing this text soon pick up on the pattern of the bunny vowing to turn into someone or something else, while his mother responds by placing herself imaginatively in the same context so she can find him. This comforting predictability is also reinforced in Brown's repetition of the same sentence structure: "If you . . . I will . . ." The pleasantly surprising aspects of the bunny's playful threats and his mother's clever responses to them balance perfectly with the predictable elements, so that the text seems fresh, even after multiple readings.

PACE

While patterned language and predictability are especially important in books for two- and three-year-olds, pace is an important feature in picture books for all age levels. The best writing we find in picture-book texts takes advantage of this unique art form by acknowledging what has been called "the drama of turning the page."

Margaret Wise Brown was so skilled at pacing picture-book texts that she could actually put a great deal of description into her books and still hold the attention of young listeners. To accomplish this, she broke her text up into meaningful segments, filled with words and images that appeal to children's senses, and used the drama of turning the page to heighten tension. Her book, *The Little Island* (written under the pseudonym Golden MacDonald), for example, deals with an encounter between a kitten, who comes to a small island with people on a picnic, and the island itself. The first ten pages of text are devoted to a description of the island before the kitten arrives. There are five pages of text dealing with a conversation between the kitten and the island and, after the kitten leaves, five more pages of description of the island by itself again. Notice how the text is broken into segments to create an appropriately undulating pace.

> *Then one day*
> *all the lobsters crawled in from the sea*
> *and hid under the rocks and ledges*
> *of the Island to shed their shells*
> *and let their new ones grow hard and strong*
> *in hiding places in the dark.*
> [turn page]
> *And the seals came barking from the north*
> *to lie on the sunny rocks*
> *and raise their baby seals.*
> [turn page]
> *And the kingfishers came from the South*
> *to build nests.*
> [turn page]
> *And the gulls laid their eggs*
> *on the rocky ledges.*
> [turn page]
> *And wild strawberries turned red.*
> *Summer had come to the little Island.*

Each page describes a simple action of one of the natural inhabitants of the island. The author could just as easily have put the seals, kingfishers, gulls, and wild strawberries on one page, but instead she took her

94

time, drawing the description out over four double-page spreads. This has the effect of giving young listeners a sense of natural activity amid the soothing peacefulness of the island.

Due to the manner in which books are manufactured, the number of pages in any hardcover book is always divisible by eight. Most picture books are thirty-two pages long, though we occasionally see picture books that are forty or forty-eight pages. The writer must work within these confines. In the standard thirty-two-page book, there will generally be fifteen or sixteen segments of text. Each of these segments is rather like a chapter in a novel: Something must happen to move the story along or to add to the overall mood of the book. If too much happens in one segment, however, it can throw off the pace of the story. Who hasn't had the experience of reading aloud to a young child who tires of a particular page before all the text has been read? This may be an indication of poor pacing. For that matter, who hasn't had the experience of reading a picture book silently to oneself and feeling a strong urge to turn the page before reaching the end of the segment of text? That is definitely an indication of poor pacing! If the text doesn't hold *your* attention, how do you expect it to hold the attention of a small child?

Think of this when you evaluate picture books. Do the pages seem to turn in the right places? Does the text flow naturally when you read it aloud? How does it sound? Do you notice elements of patterned language? Are there sentence or plot structures that make the story predictable?

PICTURES

Just as writers use sounds, rhythm, and words to express meaning, artists use *visual elements*. Artists must make decisions about *composition*, or how to arrange the elements on each page. They must determine which *medium* will be most effective for their work and which *style* to use. They take all these factors into consideration, in addition to thinking of the story as a sequence of pictures.

VISUAL ELEMENTS

Visual elements are the components an artist uses in creating a picture: line, shape, texture, color, and value. Most or all these elements are combined into any one picture; however, often one element will dominate an artist's work.

LINE

There are only two types of line in art and in nature: straight and curved. These lines may be thick or thin, long or short. They can move in three possible directions: horizontal, vertical, or diagonal. Artists use directional lines for different effects. When horizontal lines dominate, they give a sense of orderly action that moves from left to right. Dominant vertical lines make a picture look still and static, giving it the photographic effect of a moment captured in time. Diagonal lines suggest spontaneous action and excitement, such as that of a person rolling down a hill. Artists use line to guide the viewer's eye across the page. They may also use line to point subtly to the objects in a picture they want the viewer to look at.

SHAPE

By shape we mean a two-dimensional pattern that is a clear representation of an object (realism), a distorted but still recognizable object (abstraction), or a shape that's an unrecognizable object (nonobjective). Shapes fall into two broad categories: curved or angular. Curved shapes are used to represent objects in nature (people, animals, foliage, the moon, etc.), while angular (especially rectangular) shapes represent artificial, man-made objects (buildings, boxes, trains, books, etc.). Artists may use curved shapes for man-made objects for a desired purpose. For example, Virginia Lee Burton used curved shapes to paint the house in *The Little House* to characterize it as human and to make it look out of place in an urban environment.

TEXTURE

Texture is the nature of the surface of shapes in a picture. Texture is best determined by the sense of touch; however, artists can communicate three types of texture visually: smooth (hard), rough, and soft with the medium used to create a picture (oils, pastels, pencil, etc.) or the medium that receives it (textured paper, wood, etc.). Because texture appeals to our tactile sense, it can be used to give a strong sensual feeling to artwork.

COLOR

We can speak about color in terms of its *hue* (the name by which we distinguish it, such as "red," "blue"), its *value* (darkness or lightness of any hue, such as "dark red," "light blue"), and *chroma* (brightness or intensity). *Achromatic colors* are the shades of gray from white to black, and *monochromatic colors* are the various values of one color. *Primary* colors (red, yellow, and blue) can be mixed with each other to produce *secondary* colors (green, purple, and orange). Together they are divided into two groups. *Complementary* colors are two opposing hues such as red and green or blue and orange, while *analogous* colors are two related hues such as red and orange or green and yellow. In addition, people often speak of colors as *warm* (red, yellow, orange) or *cool* (blue, green).

VALUE

Value refers to the lightness or darkness of any color. A hue is mixed with black to give it a darker value or with white (or water) to give it a lighter value. Value is used in black-and-white illustrations to give a sense of depth and volume. In color artwork it can be used to project a mood or to represent the passage of time. When color artwork shows no variation in value, we describe it as *flat*.

COMPOSITION

An artist must carefully plan how to arrange the visual elements on a page to create the desired mood or effect. This is rarely done without a lot of thought. In fact, if you look carefully at the composition of an illustration, you can generally see several *design principles* at work. While it is entirely possible for an artist to apply any one of the following design principles to all the visual elements in a single picture, it is not necessary for him or her to do so.

DOMINANCE

Dominance gives a sense of order by drawing the eye to certain reference points in a picture. If there are several shapes in a picture, one will dominate. If there are many colors, one will be more important. Artists create dominance by:

Making more of something. If an artist wants a rough texture to dominate, for example, he will make more of the surfaces appear to be rough.

Making something larger. To make a particular shape stand out in a picture, an artist can make it appear a lot bigger than the other shapes.

Making something brighter. Even a small shape will stand out as dominant if it's more brightly colored than the shapes around it.

Giving something more value contrast. Darker objects stand out among light and lighter objects stand out among dark.

BALANCE

Balance gives a sense of comfort by making one part of the picture equal the other. A *formal*, or *symmetrical*, balance is one with an even distribution of shapes that would produce a mirrorlike image if the picture were vertically divided into two halves. An *informal*, or *asymmetrical*, balance results from an irregular distribution of shapes—for example, a large shape placed closer to the center of a picture balances a small shape placed closer to the edge. Colors can also be balanced visually: Smaller areas of bright color balance with larger areas of weaker ones.

CONTRAST

Contrast adds excitement to a picture by making an abrupt change in a visual element. An artist may contrast thin lines with thick lines, for example, or an angular shape with a rounded one.

GRADATION

Gradation adds familiarity by reflecting the sorts of gradual change we see in everyday life. A gradation in color shows the gradual change from one color to another, as we see in nature when the sun sets. Gradation in size can give the illusion of depth. Gradation in shape reflects growth and movement.

ALTERNATION

Alternation establishes a regular pattern by alternating between two or more types of the same element—for example, two thin lines alternating repeatedly with a thick line. In picture books we see this technique used most often in decorative borders. It is also used as pattern in depicting things such as wallpaper, curtains, or clothing. Because it consists of a regular repeated pattern, a lot of alternation inspires boredom; however, used judiciously, it can have a striking effect.

VARIATION

Variation makes an overall composition more complex and engaging by changing elements in line, texture, shape, color, and value.

HARMONY

Harmony gives a feeling of subtle change and continuity by repeating any of the visual elements with only a slight variation. Harmony can be used to slow down the pace without becoming static or boring.

UNITY

Unity makes the pieces of a picture fit together as a whole so that any smaller part of a picture looks like the rest of it. One way to achieve unity is to repeat or echo one element in another part of the picture.

The artistic elements and principles of design work together to express meaning in picture-book illustrations. This may range from a simple representation of characters and action in a story to a deeper psychological interpretation of meaning conveyed through mood and emotions. A critical look at any picture's components and how they are related will help you to think about an artist's intent. It will add depth to your evaluation of a picture book. Many reviewers focus on *what* happens in a picture book without paying much attention to *how* it happens. But if you understand the elements and the principles of design, you can begin to think more critically about the art in picture books, and you can articulate your observations.

When you look at an illustration, think about the elements and how they are used. What do you notice about the use of line? Does a certain type of line dominate? What effect does this have? Why did the artist strive for this effect? What do you notice about shapes? Are they mostly rounded or are they mostly angular? Does one shape dominate a picture? Why do you think the artist wants to draw your attention to this shape? How is texture used? Does it give a distinctive feeling to the scene? What colors are used? Are they warm or cool? Do they express particular emotions, such as anger (red) or serenity (blue)? How are colors balanced in the picture?

As you turn the pages of a picture book, think about the pictures as they relate to one another. Do you notice continuity or variation in the use of elements? How does this reflect the mood or the action in the story? Do the pictures follow a logical or predictable sequence? Is there a natural movement from one page to the next? Is there an overall sense of unity or harmony in the illustrations?

Finally, think about the illustrations as they fit into the book as a whole. How do they relate to the story? Do they complement, extend, or highlight the text? Do they provide crucial details that are not present in the text but are an important part of the story? Do they clarify in such a way that they take the story beyond its words?

I will demonstrate how this sort of evaluation works by using a book that is familiar to almost everyone—*Goodnight Moon*, written by Margaret Wise Brown and illustrated by Clement Hurd. On the surface, it appears to be a simple bedtime story, and yet the fact that it has persisted as a favorite book among several generations of young children suggests that there is more to it. In terms of its writing, it has all the important features mentioned in the discussion of text: patterned language, predictability, and a perfect pace. Add to that Clement Hurd's magnificent illustrations, and the whole is greater than the sum of its parts. But what exactly is it about the illustrations that make them outstanding? Or are they outstanding? Today, amid the eye-catching new picture books on the "plateau of high performance," the illustrations in *Goodnight Moon* seem to be rather plain and humble. But the elements and design principles have not changed: Good art is good art, no matter the era. Let's apply our understanding of visual elements and composition to Hurd's well-loved and familiar pictures to see what they reveal.

First, consider the challenge Hurd faced in illustrating the text of *Goodnight Moon*. Superficially, the entire story is set in the same bedroom and consists of a list of objects present in the room. But Hurd understood the text on a deeper psychological level and used his understanding to convey meaning through the illustrations. In a study of the psychology inherent in Margaret Wise Brown's picture book texts, Dr. Timothy M. Rivinus and Lisa Audet point out that the text in *Goodnight Moon* provides a means of helping the child to separate from a parent at bedtime: "What could be more in keeping with helping the child to acquire—through simple language, plot, poetry, and picture—the pleasure of separation from a parent, to the natural embrace of sleep, to the stars and the quiet night? Learning to be alone in the company of a reading parent is dress rehearsal for the real thing." If we take time to look at Clement Hurd's illustrations with a critical eye, we can see how he managed to get this sense across in his artwork as he interpreted the surface elements in the story.

Hurd sets up a predictable pattern by alternating color full-page spreads illustrating the bedroom with pages on which details from the room (a bedside table, two kittens, etc.) are shown in shades of gray. This pattern adds variety and interest, but it also serves to illuminate the theme of Brown's text, as the achromatic pages help the child viewer focus on pieces of the whole as separate entities.

The color pages illustrate essentially the same scene over and over again with subtle shifts in perspective. This lends a sense of visual harmony that slows down the pace of what would surely be a rapid-fire story if the perspective jumped around from place to place in the room. Straight horizontal lines dominate the composition, leading the viewer's eye to sweep across the page, taking in the enumerated objects in the room. These contrast with a more subtle, diagonal line emanating from a lighted lamp that points right at the restless child in his bed. The eye is also drawn to the rounded shapes that dominate the center of each picture: a large oval rug and a hearth with a burning fire. These comforting, cozy shapes fill the distance between the child and his mother, suggesting that although they are separated from each other, they are still connected.

A subtle gradation in value occurs throughout the book in the color spreads, as the room grows darker with every turn of the page. We see gradation in shape as the moon slowly moves across the night sky outside the bedroom window. Both show the natural passage of time.

Hurd also uses balance to create a sense of comfort and security. The strong horizontal line that cuts across the center of each double-page spread represents the line between the walls, which are green, and the floor, which is red. Since red and green are complementary colors, this gives the scene a formal balance. They also provide a balance between warm and cool colors, which might reflect the child's mixed emotions about bedtime.

The achromatic pages show balance as well. The initial pages balance each other by showing different objects of similar size and shape on opposing pages. To accomplish this, Hurd surrounds the objects with amorphous shapes, but as the story progresses, the shapes grow smaller and less like each other, moving from a symmetrical to an asymmetrical balance until we get to the delightfully surprising spread that places "nobody" (a blank page) opposite a bowl of mush. The next achromatic page restores perfect balance in a double-page spread that shows the comforting, familiar horizon of a clear night sky. We might ask ourselves, why did the artist do this? What effect does it have? Does it merely serve the purpose of illustrating details of the child's bedroom? Or was the artist aiming for something more? If we think about what happens to balance in the pictures and relate it to the action of the story—a child trying to delay sleep by saying good night to everything he sees in his room—we might speculate that Hurd uses the achromatic pictures to symbolize the process of falling asleep. In the beginning, everything is clear and orderly, but things gradually get smaller and more dreamlike. We sink slowly into nothingness (the blank page) and have a momentary flash of wakefulness in which we see a bowl of mush on the bedside table. In the end, sleep takes over as an endless horizon of the world outside the bedroom window.

By looking closely at just one principle then—balance—we can see that Clement Hurd's illustrations for *Goodnight Moon* not only complement the story but also actually clarify its meaning in a way that the simple words cannot. They are an integral part of the book and contribute greatly to its success over the decades. And, remarkably, they do it all without being flashy or calling attention to themselves.

MEDIA

An artist chooses a *medium*, such as paint, ink, or cut paper, to project a desired effect. Some artists feel more comfortable working with one medium and they use it in every book they illustrate. Others use different media for different books. In recent years a lot of attention has been placed on artistic media by reviewers and many have demanded more information from the publishers. In response, some publishers place a note on the book's copyright page about the medium used to create the illustrations. Interesting as these notes may be, it is not really essential to be able to distinguish between gouache and tempera paint in evaluating or commenting about art. It is more important to notice how the use of paint affects the artistic expression as a whole.

Media can be broadly broken down into *drawing, painting, print-making, collage,* and *photography*. Combinations of any two or more of these are referred to as *mixed media*. With the technological changes in printing over the past few decades, there has been more reliance on painting and less on drawing and printmaking. Drawing and printmaking emphasize the drawn line and therefore create a *linear style*; whereas paint emphasizes color and tone, a style aptly referred to as *painterly*. Both collage and photography emphasize form and volume, which gives a three-dimensional quality to the art.

Drawing

Drawing allows for a wide range of styles and expressions through the use of line and value. Lines can express emotion and movement. They can be light and humorous or heavy and serious. Value conveys depth and volume. The most common media used for drawing are:

Pen and ink: Makes strong, sure lines that create lively characters and clearly defined settings. Pen and ink is often used to draw pictures that are then colored with paint such as watercolor. Bob Graham uses pen and ink to create detailed background settings and to show a range of human expression in his picture books such as *How to Heal a Broken Wing*. Mice characters come to life with the lively pen-and-ink strokes from artist Kevin Henkes in his beloved series of books about Lilly, Owen, Julius, and Sheila Rae.

Pencil or graphite: Allows for a full range of value from light to dark to create different moods and a sense of depth. A good example of this range can be seen in the pencil illustrations of Peter McCarty in books such as *Night Driving*, by John Coy, and *Moon Plane*.

Pastel: Powder color, mixed to the desired hue with white chalk and bound with tragacanth and liquids, is solidly packed and used in a form that resembles chalk. It has a soft, opaque quality, as is apparent in Beth Peck's illustrations for *Just Like Josh Gibson*, by Angela Johnson.

Scratchboard: Rather than drawing per se, the artist uses a sharp instrument to scratch an illustration into a two-layered black-and-white or black-and-multicolored board. Beth Krommes used this technique in Susan Marie Swanson's *The House in the Night* that features stunning black-and-white illustrations with gold watercolor highlights.

PAINTING

Painting uses color above all other elements to convey meaning and emotions. Many types of paint are used in picture books. Each begins as a finely ground pigment that is mixed with a different type of liquid to form paint and, as such, has its own distinctive properties.

Gouache: Powder color mixed with an opaque white. Laura Vaccaro Seeger's vivid paintings appropriately call attention to the creative process itself in *First the Egg*, a concept book about metamorphosis that concludes with telling a story and painting a picture.

Poster paint: A coarser version of gouache because the color pigment is not as finely ground. The paintings in *Ten, Nine, Eight*, by Molly Bang, use contrasting colors to create a sense of excitement, while rounded shapes convey security.

Tempera: Powder color ground in water and mixed with an albuminous, gelatinous, or colloidal medium. Mique Moriuchi used brightly colored tempera paint on pieces of newspaper to illustrate Aileen Fisher's poem about the life cycle in *The Story Goes On*.

Watercolor: Powder color bound with gum arabic and glycerine. It is a transparent medium applied with water. By far the most popular medium among children's book artists who use paint, watercolor opens the door to a tremendous range of expression. Artists can use it to portray quiet, somber scenes or the activity in a crowded, busy place. Watercolor is an effective medium for detailed portrayals of people and animals. David Wiesner did all these things in his watercolor illustrations for *Flotsam*.

Oil paint: Powder color mixed with linseed oil. It can be applied thickly to a surface to create texture. Paul O. Zelinsky used oil paint in *Rapunzel* to capture the feeling of Italian Renaissance art.

Acrylic: Powder color mixed with water-based plastic. Like oil paint, it can be applied thickly to create a textured surface. Yuyi Morales's acrylic paintings in *Just a Minute* maintain a consistent value throughout to give them the characteristic flat appearance of folk art.

PRINTMAKING

In printmaking, the artist creates a negative, reversed image on a surface other than paper, such as wood, linoleum, cardboard, metal, or stone. The surface is then inked and pressed against paper so that the image is transferred to the paper. The very earliest children's books, illustrated with woodcut prints, date back to the sixteenth century; and we have many strong examples of the various printmaking techniques in twentieth-century picture books. With the advances in printing technology, printmaking may be classified as an endangered art form in picture books. One unfailing holdout is the artist Arthur Geisert, who continues to create stunning picture books illustrated with etchings, such as *Nursery Crimes* and *Lights Out*. Other notable recent examples of printmaking in pictures books are Mary Azarian's woodcut illustrations in *Snowflake Bentley*, by Jacqueline Briggs Martin, and Beckie Prange's woodblock prints in *Song of the Water Boatman*, by Joyce Sidman.

COLLAGE

Fragments of paper, fabric, and other material are glued to a background paper to create collage. Because the fragments are often made up of varying substances and thicknesses, collage accentuates texture. It also encourages viewers to look closely at the pieces in a composition as a whole. Steve Jenkins's cut- and torn-paper collages illustrate his dynamic picture books about animals, such as *What Do You Do with a Tail Like This?* and *Actual Size*. Jenkins uses different kinds of paper in his collages to suggest different textures. Lois Ehlert uses objects such as buttons, ribbons, and pieces of cloth for the collages in her picture books; the collages in *Leaf Man* are created completely from actual leaves, positioned on the pages to resemble different kinds of creatures. Artists Christopher Myers and Javaka Steptoe are both known for their illustrations that combine collage and painting.

PHOTOGRAPHY

Photography is frequently used as an illustration medium in nonfiction books for children. We see photography as illustration in children's picture books as well, especially in concept books by artists like Tana Hoban, Bruce McMillan, and Margaret Miller. Nina Crews combines photography and drawing to create fantastical images of a child at play in his home in *Below*, and she uses photographs to illustrate her other books as well, such as *The Neighborhood Mother Goose*. Charles R. Smith brilliantly uses a combination of color and black-and-white photographs to tell the same story from two points of view in *Loki & Alex*. Here we see the world from the dog's point of view in black and white and from the child's in full color.

DIGITAL ART

While it's obvious that most picture books with photographs as illustration use some degree of digital manipulation, it's not always easy to tell when this is the case with other media. Prominent picture book artists Don and Audrey Wood have been outspoken about their use of digital art since 1996, but other artists have been less forthcoming. In fact, many artists have played down the fact that they used a computer to create their illustrations. This may be due to an overall feeling in the field that computer-generated art is somehow inferior because it is believed to take less effort. But actually computers are just another tool for the artists. In "How I Learned to Love the Computer," Lane Smith writes: "The advantages of the computer are endless for an illustrator who likes to experiment. For example, I can now build up an illustration as much as I want without overworking it."

Some picture-book art is completely computer generated, such as William Low's *Machines Go to Work*. Low used Adobe Illustrator, Adobe Photoshop, and Corel Painter to create artwork that looks hand painted. Other picture book artists use a combination of traditional media and digital manipulation. In *Don't Let the Pigeon Drive the Bus!*, Mo Willems created the cartoon drawings with pencil and then used Photoshop to color them. The same techniques were used by Kim LaFave in *Shinchi's Canoe*, by Nicola I. Campbell, but for a very different final effect. Whereas Willem's illustrations are light and comical, LaFave's are serious and somber.

STYLE

Style can refer to the features that make an individual artist's work distinctive and recognizable. It can also refer to a particular manner of artistic expression that has been developed over time that can be defined by broad characteristics. In written reviews of picture books, the identification of a particular art style can be very helpful to readers who are trying to get a sense of what the art looks like. If we read that the illustrations are abstract, for example, it can help us begin to picture them.

Realistic: Illustrations that attempt to depict things as they really look. Objects, animals, and people are shown in proper perspective and proportion. Jerry Pinkney's illustrations in his adaptation of Hans Christian Andersen's *The Ugly Duckling* are a good example of a realistic style.

Abstract: The artist deliberately distorts perspective and proportion so that objects and people are removed from reality. There are hundreds of examples of the use of abstraction in picture books. R. Gregory Christie's abstract illustrations are a perfect match for Jeron Ashford Frame's text in *Yesterday I Had the Blues*. The elongated limbs and oversized heads on his characters emphasize their emotional moods. The distorted objects and frenetic backgrounds in Yumi Heo's artwork for *Henry's First-Moon Birthday*, by Lenore Look, capture the sense of displacement a child feels after the birth of a new sibling.

Surrealistic: Realistic art that achieves a dreamlike quality or sense of unreality through unnatural or unexpected juxtapositions of objects or people. Stian Hole uses a surrealistic style brilliantly to show a young boy's doubts about the changes in his life in *Garmann's Summer*. Frida Kahlo's signature surrealistic style is echoed in Ana Juan's dreamlike illustrations in the biographical picture book, *Frida*, by Jonah Winter.

Nonobjective: Part of the contemporary art movement, nonobjective art gets away from the idea of depicting objects and people at all and instead uses color, texture, line, and shape to suggest expression and mood. This style is used infrequently in children's picture books, although you will sometimes see it used in backgrounds. Chris Raschka plays with nonobjective art in some of his picture books, including *Mysterious Thelonious*, where musical notes are matched to the values on a color wheel, and *Another Important Book*, by Margaret Wise Brown, where geometric shapes represent the ages one to five.

Impressionistic: A highly influential style developed by nineteenth-century French painters who used dabs of color to re-create a sense of reflected, or broken, light. Impressionists concerned themselves with the changing effect of light on surfaces to capture a subjective or sensory impression of a scene or object rather than a detailed depiction of reality. Maurice Sendak used this style in his artwork for *Mr. Rabbit and the Lovely Present*, by Charlotte Zolotow.

Expressionistic: An influential twentieth-century movement developed into a style that expresses the artist's personal response to the subject. It is closely related to abstract art. Since it is concerned primarily with the emotions, it is widely used in picture books. Vera Williams's *A Chair for My Mother* provides one of many examples.

Naive: Depicts scenes out of the artist's own experiences in what appears to be an untrained, awkward style. There is no depth in the pictures, and all people and objects appear flat and one-dimensional. West African artist Pierre Yves Njeng used this style in *Vacation in the Village*, a book that shows the typical daily life of children in Cameroon. Picture-book artist Barbara Cooney has used the naive art style in several books that cover the life spans of ordinary, fictional characters. For an example, see *Ox-Cart Man*, by Donald Hall.

Folk art: There are many variants in folk art style, as each is developed in a particular time and place and reflects the aesthetic values of the culture from which it comes. What they all have in common is a striking use of color, lack of perspective, the use of stylized pattern, and simple shapes. Folk art in its pure form has been used in picture books such as *Goha, the Wise Fool*, retold by Denys Johnson-Davies, that uses *khiyamiyas*, a traditional form of appliqué created by artisans in Cairo. Other artists have used styles inspired by folk art. For example, Nancy Hom based her paintings for the Hmong folktale *Nine in One, Grr! Grr!*, told by Blia Xiong, on the style used by the Hmong people in their embroidered story cloths. The style Paul Goble uses in all his retellings of Lakota folktales, such as *Iktomi and the Buzzard*, was inspired by nineteenth-century Lakota ledger art, an art tradition started by imprisoned Lakota warriors who drew detailed accounts of battles in ledger books.

Cartoon art: The artist uses fine line to create stock characters marked by exaggeration and absurdity. This style is widely used in humorous picture books that contain a lot of slapstick action. Harry Bliss, well known for his *New Yorker* cartoons, also uses cartooning in his humorous illustrations for picture books like Doreen Cronin's *Diary of a Worm*. Many artists combine it with design elements popularized in comic strips by using sequences of panels and speech balloons in their compositions. Mini Grey does this brilliantly in *Traction Man Is Here!*, a hilarious story about a boy who imagines his action figure as an action hero. Cartoon art is also frequently used to lighten a heavy subject and to put a comfortable distance between the child reader and a potentially disturbing theme. Steve Björkman uses a cartoon style effectively for this purpose in his illustrations for *I Hate English!*, Ellen Levine's story of a refugee child's difficult adjustment to life in the United States.

For every picture book, an artist chooses the medium and style he or she thinks will best serve the story. Many artists vary both medium and style from book to book: John Steptoe and Ed Young come immediately to mind as two artists whose picture books reflect an enormous versatility in both areas. Steptoe, for example, used heavy black lines and brightly colored stylized shapes to illustrate his urban tale *Stevie*, and he created detailed watercolor paintings for his retelling of an African folktale, *Mufaro's Beautiful Daughters*. Ed Young has used traditional cut paper (*The Emperor and the Kite*), pencil sketches (*High on a Hill*), pastels and watercolors (*Lon Po Po*) and collage (*Seven Blind Mice*) in styles ranging from realistic to nonobjective. Other artists choose to use the same medium and style again and again, and offer us a visual display of variations on a theme. Whatever the case, think about how the chosen medium and style work in the picture book you are evaluating. How is the media used to express the action or emotion in the story? Is it effective? Does the art style match the textual style? If not, is there a reason for this incongruity? Picture-book creators sometimes purposely contrast the visual and verbal tone in a story for the sake of irony. A direct, understated text may be illustrated with scenes filled with action and wild antics, so that the story springs from the deliberate conflict between the two, as Marla Frazee did with *A Couple of Boys Have the Best Week Ever*.

In spite of the great feeling of surprise and spontaneity we often get from them, it is important to remember that nothing ever happens accidentally in a picture book. It is a complex, carefully planned work of art that creates a satisfying interplay between text and pictures to tell a story that a small child can understand. By learning to look for the individual pieces and by developing an awareness of the techniques that are used to make them all work together, we can better understand the work as a whole so that we can clearly articulate our critical and emotional responses.

CHAPTER 6

Easy Readers and Transitional Books

It is a common misconception among many adults that picture books are the best books to give a child who is just learning to read. While it is true that some picture books have characteristics that make them accessible to beginning readers, most picture books, since they are intended to be read aloud to children, are written at a reading level that is much higher than that of a child in first grade. There are, however, books expressly written for children who are learning to read that use simple vocabulary, large typeface, and short sentences. These are called *easy readers, beginning readers*, or simply *readers*. One step up from readers is another category of books that are most commonly called *transitional books*. These books feature simple sentences and short chapters, and serve as a bridge between easy readers and longer chapter books.

Both beginning readers and transitional books are relatively new to the scene in children's trade publishing. In 1954 novelist John Hersey wrote an article in *Life* magazine in which he complained that children in public schools were failing to learn to read because their schoolbooks were bland and unchallenging. He described the characters in these primers as "abnormally courteous and unnaturally clean boys and girls" and the illustrations as uniform and insipid. "Why should [children] not have pictures that widen rather than narrow the associative richness the children give to the words they illustrate—drawings like those wonderfully imaginative geniuses among children's illustrators—Tenniel, Howard Pyle, Dr. Seuss . . . ?"

Soon after the article appeared in print, Dr. Seuss took up the challenge put forth by Hersey. He acquired a limited vocabulary list from the text book division at Houghton Mifflin and spent more than a year shaping just 237 easy-to-read words into a story. The result was the now-classic *The Cat in the Hat*, published by Random House in 1957. Although Hersey had been thinking of illustrations in particular when he cited Dr. Seuss, in the end it was the book's text that stood out as remarkable. Dr. Seuss showed that with a little creativity and a lot of hard work, engaging stories could be written with a controlled vocabulary.

The same year Harper & Row came out with *Little Bear* by Else Holmelund Minarik, the first title in its influential I Can Read series. While Seuss set the standard for excellence in writing, the I Can Read series set the standard for form. Recognizing that children learning to read are eager to feel like "big kids," Harper designed the books in their beginning reader series to look like skinny chapter books rather than picture books. *Little Bear*, in fact, is divided into four chapters that not only serve to give young readers natural stopping places for much-needed breaks from the hard work of reading but also help to build the self-esteem of children who pride themselves on reading chapters. The characteristic design of the I Can Read series was imitated by many other publishers as they launched their own beginning reader series in subsequent years, and today it is widely recognized as a standard form.

In the 1970s Arnold Lobel took beginning readers to new heights with the introduction of his Frog and Toad series. Separate volumes in this series have been cited as Honor Books by both the Newbery and the Caldecott committees, an indication of the overall excellence of the

Frog and Toad books, since beginning readers are rarely singled out as distinguished for either writing or art. Using a limited vocabulary, Lobel managed to create two distinctive characters by zeroing in on their simple interactions with each other. Their actions and reactions are often based on repetition, a device that makes the text predictable and easy to read, and also allows the author to introduce surprising, humorous elements to balance the predictability. In *Frog and Toad Are Friends*, for example, Frog asks Toad to tell him a story to cheer him up when he is sick. Toad seeks inspiration in unusual ways:

> *Then Toad went into the house*
> *and stood on his head.*
> *"Why are you standing*
> *on your head?" asked Frog.*
> *"I hope that if I stand on my head,*
> *it will help me*
> *to think of a story," said Toad.*
>
> *Toad stood on his head*
> *for a long time.*
> *But he could not think*
> *of a story to tell Frog.*
>
> *Then Toad poured a glass of water*
> *over his head.*
> *"Why are you pouring water*
> *over your head?" asked Frog.*
> *"I hope that if I pour water*
> *over my head,*

it will help me to think
of a story," said Toad.
Toad poured many glasses of water
over his head.
But he could not think
of a story to tell Frog.

Then Toad began
to bang his head
against the wall.
"Why are you banging your head
against the wall?" asked Frog.
"I hope that if I bang my head
against the wall hard enough,
it will help me to think of a story,"
said Toad.

Each of Toad's unpredictable actions is clearly shown in the illustrations. These pictures give clues to the reader who is struggling to decode the words. Throughout the Frog and Toad books, Lobel provides a comfortable context for beginning readers with both words and pictures. His words provide clues by using repetition, and his pictures provide clues by depicting action. As beginning reader books, they represent the perfect unity of form and content.

Seuss, Minarek, and Lobel set a high standard for easy readers that few have been able to meet. To encourage excellence in this sort of writing, the ALA's Association for Library Service to Children established a new award in 2004, named for Dr. Seuss. The Theodor Seuss Geisel Award recognizes both the author and illustrator of a book for beginning readers. Interestingly, it is not limited to books in an easy-reader format; it can also be awarded to a picture book that is easy enough for a child just learning to read.

Unfortunately there has not been a similar progression in the development of books written for children at the next stage in their reading. Parents, teachers, and librarians had for a long time been stressing a need for what they called "third grade books"—books that offered a little more challenge than the hardest easy readers and yet were still a bit easier than the easiest chapter books. Children who were making the transition from easy readers to chapter books were beginning to read mainly for meaning, and yet reading was still hard work for their untrained eyes. They needed books that struck a delicate balance between readers and chapter books. Although most publishers' lists offered at least a few titles that fit into this category, there was no consistent effort to create this type of book specifically until the mid-1980s.

An outstanding forerunner of transitional books, and one that many hoped would set the standard, was Ann Cameron's *The Stories Julian Tells*. This easy chapter book featuring an imaginative young African-American boy and his trusting, gullible little brother, Huey, was perfectly designed for children making the transition from easy readers to chapter books. Like many easy readers, it has a large typeface and the number of lines per page never exceeds fifteen. But *The Stories Julian Tells* is designed to look like a thick chapter book, the sort of book that readers making the transition are desperate to be able to read. Many librarians who have had the opportunity to introduce these young readers to Julian have seen this scene played out again and again: As the librarian pulls the book off the shelf, the child hesitates upon seeing its thickness. The moment the book is opened, however, the child shows visible relief, then delight, then pride. Because adults saw this happen repeatedly with a variety of young readers, soon after *The Stories Julian Tells* was published, they asked for several dozen more like it.

A few years later when publishers began to develop series to meet these demands, *The Stories Julian Tells* and its follow-up, *More Stories Julian Tells*, were not used as models, unfortunately. Publishers opted instead for a standard design that made the books look like skinny chapter books. In order to accomplish this, more text had to be crammed onto each page by using smaller type and more lines per page. Even subsequent volumes in Cameron's Julian series adopted this new look, rather than following the standard for excellence set by the first two books in the series.

The success of both easy readers and transitional books is as much dependent on form as it is on content. Because these books are created especially to meet the needs of children who are developing reading skills, it is helpful for us to have a minimal basic understanding of what happens when a child begins to read so that we can apply this knowledge to these books when we evaluate them. Most children learn to read in the controlled setting of a classroom, and they have traditionally been taught using basal readers that are specially designed for this purpose. Easy readers and transitional books were not specifically created to replace the basal reader; rather, they were intended as supplementary reading so that children can practice newly acquired skills and find a wide range of reading material that interests them.

Children who are beginning to read are learning to decode printed symbols that stand for words within their oral vocabulary. To decode the words, they sound them out or say them aloud so that they can hear them. As children learn to read, they develop a store of *sight words*, common words that they learn to recognize immediately, such as "the," "ball," "mother," "play," and "run." Sight words are most often purposefully taught in the classroom, thus we get the concept of "reading at grade level."

Part of the challenge children face is in training their eyes to move from left to right across lines of print. The eye is controlled by small muscle movements, and for children small muscle movements are a challenge in and of themselves. When the eyes move across a line of print, they make a series of jumps, stopping briefly to focus. An experienced adult reader typically sees two letters to the left side of the point of focus and six to eight letters to the right. The inexperienced child reader, however, sees one letter to the left and one letter to the right of their point of focus. This physical reality explains why children learning to read find it easier to decode words made up of fewer than five letters. As their eye muscles begin to develop, they are gradually able to take in more on the right side of the point of focus and they can handle longer, unfamiliar words. They can also begin to handle longer sentences. All the while, they continue to add to their store of sight words. All these factors work together, so that with practice children eventually can make a shift from reading aloud to decode the words to reading silently for meaning.

The creators of easy readers and transitional books have taken this process into account in developing their books. They strive to meet the needs of children who are learning to read by paying special attention to both content and design. As we evaluate these books, we should look carefully at the following components of each.

Content: How is the story written to make it easy to read? What sort of vocabulary did the author choose to use? How often are difficult words used, and how does the author use them? How long are the sentences? Are the sentences simple, compound, or complex? How does the author use structure to build context and provide textual clues? How do the illustrations support the text and offer help to the reader?

Design: How is the text presented to make it easy to read? Is the type large and clear? Is there a lot of white space on the page? How long are the lines of type, and how many lines appear on the page? How often do illustrations appear, and how much space do they cover?

EASY READERS

When we evaluate easy readers, it is important to think about them in terms of what the author and illustrator have created (content) and how the publisher has presented the work of the author and illustrator (design). Both aspects should be given equal importance by the critic. In the best examples of this type of book, content and design form a unified whole that makes the task of reading easier and thus pleasurable for the child.

CONTENT

VOCABULARY

Many easy readers are written using the sight words children learn in first and second grade, combined with short words that are easy to decode. Compound words composed of two short sight words, such as "snowball," are also easier to read. Longer, unfamiliar words can be successfully integrated in moderation if there are strong context clues in the pictures or if they are used as descriptors that can be skipped without losing meaning. In looking at the words appearing in easy readers, think about the kinds of words that are used. Are they sight words? If not, have they fewer than five letters? If they are long words, how are they used? Are there picture clues to help the child figure them out? Are the words likely to be part of the child's natural oral language? A word of three or four letters, such as "rue" or "cusp," isn't likely to mean anything to a six-year-old, even if it can be decoded. Notice the way Dr. Seuss ingeniously uses short words and sight words in this passage from *The Cat in the Hat*:

> *"Now look what you did!"*
> *Said the fish to the cat.*
> *"Now look at this house!*
> *Look at this! Look at that!*
> *You sank our toy ship,*

Sank it deep in the cake.
You shook up our house
And you bent our new rake."

SENTENCE LENGTH

Children who are concentrating more on decoding the words than on
the words' meaning need short, declarative sentences, so that they haven't
forgotten the beginning of the sentence by the time they reach the end
of it. Sentences made up of five words are ideal for children just beginning to read, but those who are gaining skill and confidence can handle
up to ten words per sentence. Even for more competent young readers,
however, look for sentences of alternating lengths. An author may, for
example, follow a long sentence by a succession of short sentences, as
Dori Chaconas does in *Cork & Fuzz*:

Cork bent down and wiggled Fuzz's tail.
Fuzz did not move.
Cork wiggled Fuzz's nose.
He wiggled Fuzz's foot.
Fuzz did not move.

Occasionally longer sentences can be used successfully, if they can be
broken up naturally into lines of shorter length as in this sentence from
Little Bear:

So Little Bear begins to make soup
in the big black pot.

Longer sentences can also work when a writer builds textual context
using repetition, as Arnold Lobel did in the passage quoted earlier from

Frog and Toad Are Friends or when a writer uses rhyme, as Dr. Seuss did in *The Cat in the Hat*. Both these devices serve to make the text more predictable and therefore easier to read.

In easy readers, sentence length and structure are just as important as the vocabulary used to tell the story. When you evaluate this type of book, look at the sentences. How many words appear in them? If long sentences are used, are they preceded or followed by short ones? Do you notice a lot of commas in the text? If so, this is often an indication of dependent clauses or extra information that makes the text harder to read. "Sam, a mean dog, bit my sister" is much more difficult to read than "Sam was a mean dog. He bit my sister."

PLOT

Beyond the constraints of language, easy readers fall into a broad range of categories, including nonfiction, folklore, poetry, science fiction, mysteries, historical fiction, animal fantasies, and realistic fiction, although the latter two make up the majority of what has been published to date.

The first page or two of an easy reader is especially important because it must establish the context and stir children's interest enough to draw them into the story.

Ruth Horowitz uses simple words and short sentences to introduce characters and setting in the opening two pages of *Breakout at the Bug Lab*:

> *Our mom works in a bug lab.*
> *She collects robber flies.*
> *They carry their food with their feet.*
> *She looks at dung beetles.*
> *They eat animal poop!*

But the best bug in her lab is Max.
Max is Mom's pet cockroach.
Max comes from an island near Africa.
He loves fruit and hates bright lights.
Max is as big as a bite-sized candy bar.
He hisses like a snake when he is mad.

Note the word choices and sentence structure the author uses to describe an unfamiliar setting and an unusual character. She succeeds in making the text accessible by beginning with easy words and sentences that are sure to pique the interest of young children. This gives young readers the confidence they need to keep reading. Look closely at the first two or three pages of an easy reader as you evaluate it. Does it begin by using short sentences and simple concepts? Does it establish the setting and introduce the subject or characters quickly? Is it likely to make children want to turn the pages and keep reading?

Most stories in easy readers involve two or three main characters and have fast-moving plots with clear, direct action. Descriptive passages and internal motives are kept to a minimum. Many follow the pattern established by the I Can Read series and break the story up into four to six chapters. When this is done, chapters should be episodic; in other words, the action started at the beginning of a chapter is completed—brought to some sort of resolution—at the end of the chapter. Each chapter then functions as a short story; and taken as a whole, all the chapters that make up one book have characters and setting in common.

Each of the four chapters in Minarik's *Little Bear* deals with the playful interactions between a mother bear and her small son. In chapter 1, Little Bear wants to go out to play in the snow, but he keeps returning to tell his mother he is cold and needs something warm to put on. She gives him a hat, a coat, and a pair of snow pants before suggesting he remove them all and wear his own nice warm fur coat outside. In chapter 2, Little Bear prepares a special birthday soup for himself as a succession of guests arrives for his party. Each one asks him what he is cooking, giving him an opportunity to describe repeatedly the wonders of birthday soup before Mother Bear comes home with a surprise birthday cake. In both of these chapters, episodes are built on a predictable accumulation of repeated actions that pave the way for a satisfying surprise ending. The character of an inventive and slightly dependent Little Bear is firmly established through his interactions with his patient, loving mother. After the first two chapters, young readers will feel familiar enough with the characters of Little Bear and his mother so that they can easily follow the two final chapters that break away from the predictable pattern of repetition. Like the first two chapters, chapters 3 and 4 center on Little Bear's actions, which elicit calm and satisfying reactions from his mother.

To evaluate the storyline in an easy reader, look at each double-page spread and notice what happens. There should be some action on every page. Are action verbs used to move the plot along? Are characters developed through interaction? Does the author use repeated actions in a creative way? Are surprises balanced with predictable elements?

ILLUSTRATIONS

Pictures in easy readers appear on every double-page spread, and they generally vary in size from page to page. In addition to illustrating the story, they can give essential clues to help out with words or concepts that young readers may find difficult. When Cynthia Rylant tells us in *Henry and Mudge: The First Book* that the puppy Mudge grew out of seven collars in a row, artist Suçie Stevenson illustrates the seven collars and shows them in succession. This single illustration gives clues about the word "collar" and the concepts "grew out of" and "in a row." It also suggests just how big the tiny puppy grew to be so that readers are prepared for a surprise when they see and read about the huge dog Mudge on the following page.

DESIGN

Because easy readers must meet the physical as well as intellectual needs of children who are learning to read, it is especially important to pay attention to design factors such as size of typeface, line length, space between words, space between lines, number of lines per page, amount of white space per page, and placement of illustrations.

SIZE OF TYPEFACE

Typography has its own system of measurement based on *points*. A point is a little less than 1/72 of an inch. Most books for adults are set in typeface that measures 10 or 12 points in height. The standard size typeface for beginning readers is 18 points.

10 points

12 points

18 points

LINE LENGTH

By line length we mean the number of words per line. A line may be a complete sentence, or it may be a phrase. Beginning readers should have lines between two and ten words in length. The longer the line, the more difficult it is for children to read. When you look at lines, you should also pay attention to where new sentences begin. New sentences beginning at the end of a line are harder for children to read than those that start at the beginning of a line. Line breaks usually come at a natural place to pause, and the right margins are not justified.

Space Between Words

For inexperienced readers the space between words is just as important as the period at the end of the sentence is for experienced readers. They "read" the space as an indication of where one word ends and the next word begins. Spaces between words should be wide and distinct.

Space Between Lines

There should be plenty of space between lines (*leading*, so called because old typesetting technology used strips of lead between the lines of type) in beginning readers so that a child can easily keep his or her place in a line without wandering down into the next line. The more space between lines, the easier the text is to read. Most often, leading is equal to the type size—that is, if the type size is 18 point, there are 18 points of space between lines.

Number of Lines per Page

Due to illustrations, this will vary from page to page but in easy readers, the number of lines per page should not exceed fifteen.

Amount of White Space per Page

Children work hard to decode the text in easy readers, and they need to rest their eyes frequently. A lot of white space around words and pictures gives their eyes a place to rest.

Placement of Illustrations

In easy readers illustrations appear on every double-page spread. They may give essential picture clues to help the child, and they may provide little breaks for the eyes. They should not overwhelm the reader by covering up every bit of white space, nor should they confuse the reader by taking over the text's territory. They are there to complement the text, not compete with it.

LEVELS

Easy readers fall roughly into three levels based on how easy or difficult they are for children to read. In evaluating an easy reader, it is very important for the critic to determine the level of the book by looking at elements of design and content. Although there are no hard-and-fast rules—and even formal readability scales such as Frye and Spache are not always reliable—we can make a general overall assessment of a book by taking concrete factors such as word usage, line length, sentence structure, and illustrations into consideration.

LEVEL ONE

The very easiest of the easy readers are written at a first-grade level. The text is set in 17- to 20-point type; and there are, on average, five words per line. The sentences average five to seven words, and the words that are used are largely sight vocabulary or one-syllable words of five letters or fewer. There are generally two to seven lines per page, with as much as two thirds of each page used for illustrations and white space. The illustrations provide plenty of picture clues.

Mo Willems's popular Elephant & Piggie series falls into this category. All the text in these books appears in color-coded dialogue bubbles as the story is built with a conversation between the two characters and the accompanying illustrations that offer strong picture clues. In *There Is a Bird on Your Head*, for example, Piggie and readers can see exactly what is going on as two birds build a nest and lay eggs on top of Elephant's head. Elephant, however, must rely on Piggie to tell him what is happening:

"Is there a
bird on my
head now?"
"No.
Now there are two
birds on your head."
"What are two birds
doing on my head?"
"They are in love!"
"The birds on my
head are in love?"
"They are
love birds!"
"Love birds!
How do you
know they are
love birds?"
"They are
making
a nest!"

Like Willems, David Milgrim excels at writing humorous books at this level, such as *See Pip Point*, one in a series about two friends, a robot and a mouse. Milgrim brilliantly uses sight vocabulary to parody basal readers, a technique that works because of the strong context provided through his illustrations. For example, a picture showing Pip the mouse being lifted high off the ground after he's been handed a helium balloon reads:

See Pip go up.
See Pip go way up.

See Pip go up, up,
and away.

Written at a second-grade level, easy readers in the middle range begin to use slightly more complex sentences, alternating them with short simple ones. The number of sight words has greatly expanded, and children can now handle occasional unfamiliar multisyllabic words that are part of their natural oral speech. No more than five words per line continues to be the ideal length, even though the sentences themselves can be longer. The number of lines per page varies from four to fifteen, and the text is fairly evenly balanced with illustrations or white space.

Erica Silverman's Cowgirl Kate and Cocoa series provides a good example of books at this level. They deal with the humorous friendship between a cowgirl and her talking horse, Cocoa. Here's a typical exchange between them from the first volume in the series, *Cowgirl Kate and Cocoa*:

> *She went to the tallest tree*
> *and started to climb.*
> *Up she went,*
> *higher*
> *and higher*
> *and higher.*
> *Cocoa galloped over.*
> *"Come down, please!" he cried.*
> *"I do not want you to fall."*
>
> *"Don't worry," said Cowgirl Kate.*
> *"I am a good climber."*

"And I am a good worrier," said Cocoa.
"Please come down!"

The most challenging of the easy readers are written at a level that is typical of children who are beginning third grade. Due to the use of more difficult words, an adult reading the text may not even be aware that the book is written with a controlled vocabulary. There is a greater frequency of compound and complex sentences, resulting in language that begins to sound more natural. Still, the line lengths are short, fewer than eight words, and the number of lines per page does not exceed fifteen. The text may cover up to three quarters of the page, although due to the large type and plenty of space between lines, there is a lot of white space on each page. Illustrations may even appear only on alternating pages, and they begin to function more as decorations.

Note the characteristics of a level three reader in this passage from *Mercy Watson Goes for a Ride*, by Kate DiCamillo:

Officer Tomilello had to go very fast
to catch up with the convertible.
The officer had to speed.
"Is that vehicle swerving?" Officer
Tomilello asked himself.
"It is," he answered himself. "It is
most definitely swerving."
"Is the driver of that vehicle breaking
the law?" Officer Tomilello asked.

"Without a doubt," he answered,
"the law is being broken. It is time to

take action."
Officer Tomilello pulled up
alongside the car. He shouted into
his bullhorn: "PULL OVER!"

Children who are comfortably reading level three texts are probably ready to make the jump to the next highest level: the transitional book. This stage in a child's reading life is usually brief, but it is very important. It is during this stage that the child gains confidence and discovers that reading is personally important and pleasurable.

TRANSITIONAL BOOKS

As noted earlier, there has not been the careful attention given to the design of transitional books as there has to easy readers. Ann Cameron's *The Stories Julian Tells* sets a standard for excellence in design that few have matched (or even striven for). Like easy readers, it has a large typeface and the number of lines per page never exceeds fifteen. The number of words per line, however, has been increased to an average of eight to twelve. Sentences are no longer broken down into shorter lines, and right-hand margins are now justified. There is plenty of white space on every page, with generous margins at the top, bottom, and sides; and there is still a full line of leading between every line of type. The book includes frequent full-page black-and-white illustrations, but there may be two or three double-page spreads in a row with no illustrations at all. The six chapters are short and episodic, varying in length from seven to seventeen pages. It is the length of the chapters, the justified right margins, and the smaller ratio of text to illustrations that give *The Stories Julian Tells* the look of a chapter book, while design elements—such as line length, type size, and white space—make it accessible to inexperienced readers.

Compare the first to the third book in the Julian series, *Julian's Glorious Summer*. The latter was designed to conform to the publisher's then-new transitional series, Stepping Stone. The third Julian book uses a much smaller typeface and has up to twenty-five lines per page. This design is much more typical of what we see in most publishers' series of transitional books.

There are several other characteristics these books have in common that make them more accessible to newly independent readers.

A simple vocabulary without too many surprising descriptors or multisyllabic words. Children at this stage of reading are beginning to read for meaning, so it is important that the words they are reading mean something to them. What words has the author used? Are they common, everyday words a seven- or eight-year-old is likely to know? If the meaning of a word is likely to be unfamiliar, has the author provided a context that will give clues to the reader?

Ann Cameron included a chapter about a fig tree in *The Stories Julian Tells*. While transitional readers would not have any trouble reading the word "fig," Cameron must have been aware that there would be some children who had never seen or eaten a fig. Notice how skillfully she provides a context for those children so that they will not be excluded:

> *In the summer I like to lie in the grass and look at clouds and eat figs. Figs are soft and purple and delicious. Their juice runs all over my face, and I eat them till I'm so full I can't eat anymore.*

Sentences that are relatively short, direct, and uncomplicated. Pay close attention to sentence length. Do long sentences alternate with short ones? How are longer sentences constructed? Compound sentences are easier to read, and complex sentences with dependent clauses are more difficult. Do you see more than a few commas per page? If so, that may be an indication that more complicated sentences are being used, as commas often set off dependent clauses.

Compare the following passages. The first is from Lenore Look's *Ruby Lu, Brave and True* and the second from Anne Fine's *The Jamie and Angus Stories*:

> *Tiger was Ruby's best friend. He lived two blocks away, but it felt like he lived next door. He was faster than e-mail. "Don't break the speed limit!" his mother always called after him. He was also fast at making friends. With just the right smile, he was always saying hi and having a chat. Ruby didn't make friends so quickly. She liked her old friends best.*

> *Jamie sighed. Angus was looking at him most forlornly. He'd had a boring time alone at home, and now, instead of being cuddled and talked to and offered his very own SpaghettiO to balance on his nose, he was going to have to carry on standing by the plate rack, all alone, watching Jamie struggle through some fancy supper with olives.*

Even though the passage from *The Jamie and Angus Stories* uses relatively simple vocabulary, the sentence structure is quite complex and would require the skills of a more experienced reader. Because this sort of complexity is common in the book, we would not classify it as a book for transitional readers, even though it has many of the characteristics we look for: large, clear typeface; plenty of white space; occasional illustrations; and short, episodic chapters.

Brief episodes, chapters, or intervals that stand out to the reader. The average length of a chapter in a transitional book is just six to eight pages. Each chapter typically follows the actions of one, two, or three characters in one place at one time. All the chapters in Michelle Edwards's *Pa Lia's First Day*, for example, take place during a single day at school and introduce the classmates who are main characters in the Jackson Friends series. *Runaway Radish*, by Jessie Haas, takes place over a long period of time as it follows the life of a horse and its owners, but each chapter is limited to one main episode that moves the plot along. These episodes can be described in short sentences, for example:

Chapter 1: We meet Radish and his first owner, Judy.

Chapter 2: We meet Radish's second owner, Nina.

Chapter 3: Radish tries to follow Nina when she takes another horse out for a ride, and he gets lost.

Chapter 4: Together Nina and Judy find Radish.

Chapter 5: Radish is given to a riding camp where, years later, Judy's daughter learns to ride.

Look at each chapter to see exactly what happens. Can it be easily summed up in a few words? If not, it will probably be too difficult for transitional readers.

Inexperienced readers often have a great deal of trouble grasping jumps in time and changes in setting. These are two very important techniques in fiction writing, and children need to gain familiarity with them in order to become competent readers of fiction. Because chapters are short in transitional books, changes in time and setting generally occur between rather than within chapters. These changes will not be obvious to young readers unless they are given clear, direct descriptions. Phrases such as "The next day . . ." and "When Sam got to the park . . ." are essential.

In *Berta: A Remarkable Dog*, Celia Barker Lottridge always lets her readers know exactly where and when the action takes place by building it into the opening sentence of each chapter. For example:

Chapter 1: *"Berta lived in the small town of Middle Westfield in a yellow house with a barn behind it."*

Chapter 2: *"It was March, a bothersome month in Middle Westfield."*

Chapter 3: *"The chicks were still living in the storeroom when Mr. Miller burst through the back door early the next Saturday morning with a wide grin on his face."*

Chapter 4: *"Marjory was walking slowly home from school."*

Chapter 5: *"By the next Saturday every hint of spring was gone."*

Look for changes in time and setting. Where and how often do they occur? Does the author use helpful descriptive phrases to let readers know exactly where and when the action takes place?

Content compelling enough to hold a child's interest but not so complicated that it's hard to follow. Like easy readers, transitional books generally have two or three main characters and brisk plots with a lot of action. Contemporary stories about friends and family work especially well, because the types of characters, situations, and conflicts they offer are familiar and easily understood by newly independent readers. More whimsical elements can be introduced if they are firmly rooted in a reality that children will easily absorb. Marion Dane Bauer's *The Blue Ghost* introduces supernatural elements, but they are firmly grounded in the familiar reality of a family summer cottage.

Children who are going through this stage in their lives as readers need to build self-confidence as they make the leap from easy readers to chapter books. Transitional books serve as a bridge for them. It is a bridge that some children will cross very quickly; others will have to linger for a while. The best transitional books will suggest that the trip across is worth it and that great things await them on the other side.

CHAPTER 7

Fiction

Children's fiction offers a rich diversity of style, content, and form to satisfy a variety of tastes, interests, and abilities of young readers. From the witty portrayals of ordinary child life in Beverly Cleary's Ramona books to Gary Paulsen's gripping stories of wilderness survival to the complexities of character revealed in Virginia Hamilton's multilayered novels, there are books to amuse, stimulate, and captivate many types of readers.

With such a wide range of fiction, how do we choose the best? What characterizes an outstanding novel for children? Are there literary standards that we can apply to all works of fiction? How can we tell what will appeal to children at different age levels and abilities? Can a fourth grader read the same books as a seventh grader? Do boys and girls like the same kinds of books? How important is popularity and child appeal? Why don't they give the Newbery Medal to popular books? What's the problem with formula series books, anyway? If kids are reading them, isn't that the most important thing?

These are all questions commonly asked by people who are thinking about children's fiction. All are valid and important questions for us to consider. Many of them have their roots in the conflicting points of view that led to the creation of contemporary children's fiction in the first place.

Prior to the 1920s, most of children's fiction consisted of popular series books, such as Tom Swift, the Motor Girls, the Bobbsey Twins, and dozens of other series written according to a prescribed formula. There were no separate children's divisions in publishing houses at the time, and even children's departments in public libraries were a rarity.

In the early part of the twentieth century libraries began to establish specialized departments for children by hiring women who had been trained in a newly developing field devoted to children's services. But when these librarians looked for books to add to their library's collections, they found that there was little that met their critical standards. In 1920 Anne Carroll Moore, the influential head of New York Public Library's Office of Work with Children, lamented: "We are tired of substitutes for realities in writing for children. The trail . . . [is] strewn with patronage and propaganda, moralizing self-sufficiency and sham efficiency, mock heroics and cheap optimism—above all, with the commonplace in theme, treatment, and language."

Of course, there were books such as *The Adventures of Tom Sawyer*, *Little Women*, and *Hans Brinker; or, The Silver Skates*, but these titles were the exception, not the rule. Thanks to the combined efforts of children's librarians, publishers, and booksellers, the rules were about to change.

In the United States just after the end of World War I, great changes were in the air. Within a five year period (1919 to 1924) there was a remarkable series of events that would have a long-lasting impact: Children's divisions were set up in publishing houses; *The Horn Book* magazine was founded; Children's Book Week was established; and perhaps, most important, the Newbery Medal was created to encourage writers and publishers to produce high-quality books for children.

Of course, this radical change in children's books was not without its opponents. The proponents and producers of formula series books launched a verbal attack on children's librarians, claiming that, since they were mere women (and spinsters, at that), they had no right to judge what was fit reading for red-blooded American boys. Librarians, in alliance with the Boy Scouts of America, countered by emphasizing "good books for boys" in their early recommendations, thus advancing the notion of gender-specific reading tastes.

The first several winners of the Newbery Medal are a case in point. They are for the most part titles that would be touted as books for boys. Speaking about the work of 1924 Newbery Medalist Charles Boardman Hawes (*The Dark Frigate*) shortly after the announcement had been made, librarian Louise P. Latimer stated: "Let us nail them to our mast and say to those who question or discredit our judgment, these are examples of good writing for boys. Match them with hack writing if you can."

Children's librarians quickly established themselves as the major influence in setting the literary standards for children's fiction. Formula series fiction faded into the background, and although it has never completely died out, it has been greatly marginalized in school and public libraries.

LITERARY GENRES

Over the past several decades a significant body of outstanding fiction written especially for children has developed. It can be categorized by genres and subgenres, and it's important for a critic to identify the genre of any book under consideration.

REALISM

Realism is most easily defined as stories that could happen in the real world. This is an extremely popular form of children's fiction with both authors and readers. Realism itself can be divided into the following sub-categories.

Contemporary realistic fiction: Stories set in the here and now. They can deal with serious issues, such as Kevin Henkes's evocative *Bird Lake Moon*, in which two boys are dealing with loss in their families, or they can be funny stories like Megan McDonald's Judy Moody series.

Historical fiction: Stories set in the past. Setting is generally integral. The author must bring unfamiliar events and everyday experiences to life and offer enough historical context for child readers so that they understand the time period. The author must also remain true to the historical era about which he or she is writing. Karen Cushman is a master at writing compelling books set in the past, such as *The Midwife's Apprentice*, set in the Middle Ages, and *The Loud Silence of Francine Green*, set just after World War II.

School stories: For obvious reasons, this subgenre is unique to children's and young adult literature. Traditionally, school stories were set in boarding schools, and the setting served as a microcosm for society at large; but today we see many children's novels set in public school classrooms, where the teacher, classmates, and occasionally the principal are the main characters. In *The Fabled Fourth Graders of Aesop Elementary School*, Candace Fleming pits a rambunctious group of nine-year-olds against a resourceful teacher. A classroom of fifth graders take a vow of silence in Andrew Clements's *No Talking*, with hilarious results.

Sports stories: Stories that feature a child or sometimes an entire team playing a specific sport. The best books in this genre have plenty of descriptive passages that make play-by-play action an integral part of the plot. Matt Christopher set the standard for children's sports fiction, and his books continue to be favorites with young sports enthusiasts. Many sports novels follow the experiences of one player or team, perfecting skills to prepare for the big game, but there are exceptions to this formula. The entire story of *Six Innings: A Game in the Life*, by James Preller, takes place during a Little League championship game, told from the different points of view of the players.

Survival stories: Stories that tell of a character's struggle to survive, either physically or emotionally. In most survival stories, characters must make life-or-death decisions that determine their fate. *Run, Boy, Run*, by Uri Orlev, is a Holocaust survival story in which an eight-year-old boy escapes from the Warsaw Ghetto and must survive on his own. In Helen Frost's *Diamond Willow*, a twelve-year-old girl must survive on her own when she is trapped in a snowstorm during what should have been a two-hour dogsled ride. These novels show both the physical and emotional survival of the main characters.

FANTASY AND SCIENCE FICTION

While fantasy and science fiction are sometimes classed together, they are each distinctive subgenres in their own right. What they have in common and what distinguishes them from realistic fiction is that they do not take place in the real world as we know it.

Fantasy: Stories that take place in an imaginary world created by the author. The author creates the rules by which the world operates and must remain consistent to them. He or she must also make the world believable enough that readers will be able to suspend disbelief when they enter it. Fantasy is further subdivided into *high fantasy* and *low fantasy*. High fantasy is set in a completely imaginary world. A good example is *Princess Academy*, by Shannon Hale, set in an imaginary kingdom where villagers are able to communicate telepathically. Low fantasy is set in the real world but introduces magical elements. Ingrid Law's *Savvy* is set in the contemporary United States but features a family whose members have a magical power that is revealed on their thirteenth birthdays. Low fantasies often set up parallel imaginary worlds that coexist with our real world. Examples are the Gregor series, by Suzanne Collins; the Percy Jackson and the Olympians series, by Rick Riordan; and J. K. Rowling's Harry Potter series. *Animal fantasies* are another popular subcategory for children. These range from stories such as Brian Jacques's Redwall series, in which mice and other animals stand in for human characters, to stories like *Masterpiece*, by Elise Broach, in which humans interact with talking animals—in this case, beetles.

Science fiction: Sometimes called *speculative fiction*, these are stories set in an imaginary world that operates by the laws of science, rather than by magic. Children's science fiction often deals with ethical issues by taking some aspect of contemporary life and projecting it into a future time. *The Hunger Games*, by Suzanne Collins, for example, depicts a bleak future in which a single reality television show determines the fate of entire populations represented by the contestants. The ethics of cloning, and nature versus nurture, are both central to the theme of Nancy Farmer's *The House of the Scorpion*, when a boy learns he is the clone of an evil 142-year-old dictator.

OTHER GENRES IN CHILDREN'S FICTION

Horror: Stories that set out to scare the reader. This is an especially popular genre with many children, something that many adults find puzzling. But the attraction of most horror for children is that they can identify with the central theme, which is powerlessness, and find comfort in seeing a child facing his fears and overcoming more powerful forces, such as zombies, vampires, and psycho killers. Neil Gaiman's *Coraline* is a good example of a deliciously scary novel in which a young girl outwits evil predators who look exactly like her parents, except for their button eyes.

Mystery: Stories in which some sort of mystery or puzzle is introduced early on that gets children involved in trying to figure out what has happened. Mysteries include detective stories, suspense novels, and tales of the supernatural; and they are marked by suspense and fast-paced action. There are excellent children's mystery series with child detectives, such as the Echo Falls series, by Peter Abrahams, and the Enola Holmes series, by Nancy Springer. In Rebecca Stead's *When You Reach Me*, mysterious notes left for the main character by an unknown person provide both the puzzle and the clues needed to solve it.

ILLUSTRATED NOVELS

In the first half of the twentieth century, most children's novels were accompanied by illustrations, either in black and white or as full-color plates tipped in between pages of text. In the late 1950s, illustrations in chapter books fell out of favor, and within ten years it was a rarity to see them in a children's novel. But at the beginning of the twenty-first century, they have been making a comeback and are once again becoming common, even in books for teenagers.

Most illustrated children's novels use art as decoration, either as chapter headings as we see in Louise Erdrich's *The Birchbark House,* or as occasional full-page illustrations, such as those created by Bagram Ibatoulline for Kate DiCamillo's *The Miraculous Journey of Edward Tulane.* In some cases, the illustrations are an integral part of the book. A notable example is Brian Selznick's *The Invention of Hugo Cabret*, a novel that opens with 21 wordless illustrated double-page spreads and includes 284 pages of illustrations throughout its 533 pages. So integral are the illustrations to the story, in fact, the book won the 2008 Caldecott Medal for distinguished illustration, marking the first time a novel had been recognized in this way.

Another popular form of illustrated children's fiction is the *graphic novel* that uses sequential art and words in accordance with comic-book conventions to tell a story. While graphic novels are especially popular with teenagers, many publishers are beginning to develop graphic novel lines for children, as well. Jennifer and Matthew Holm's superb Babymouse series is perfect for elementary-school-aged children, as is Kean Soo's *Jellaby*.

When evaluating the illustrations in children's fiction, you can consider some of the same questions you would ask yourself about picture book illustrations. In addition, you should consider them in the context of the novel itself. How well do the illustrations match the tone of the book? Are they age appropriate and likely to appeal to child readers, or do they make the book look babyish? Will they make the book more accessible to reluctant readers? Do they detract from or contradict the text? Are they integral to the story, and, if so, how do they enhance it?

Many children develop an early preference for a particular genre, and read almost exclusively in that genre when they read for pleasure, right up into adulthood. One of the reasons for the broad popularity of the Harry Potter series, in fact, is that it crosses into just about every literary genre in children's literature and thus appeals to a very broad range of readers.

Although each category of children's fiction has its own special qualities, and some—most notably fantasy and science fiction—have their own rules and standards for excellence, there are certain elements they all have in common. When we evaluate any type of children's fiction, we can look closely at plot, characterization, point of view, setting, style, and theme.

PLOT

The basis of all fiction is the *plot*, that is, a series of events that tell the story, actions that are linked by cause and effect, so that the pieces of the story are all tied together by a narrative. Unlike real life, everything that happens in a story has a recognizable purpose. If, for example, a notebook is left on the school bus in the first chapter, we know that something is going to happen as a result; otherwise, the author wouldn't have mentioned it.

NARRATIVE STRUCTURE

Narrative order refers to the sequence in which the events take place. Most children's novels follow a direct linear pattern, with events occurring in *chronological order*. They may take place over a period of just a few days, a month, or years. *The Birchbark House* provides a good example of a straightforward, progressive plot. The story follows young Omakayas over the course of a year, and readers can see how she and her family adapted to seasonal changes in their environment, contrasted with the change brought on by a stranger entering their community.

A slightly more complex form of narrative order based on chronology is one that tells the story from the point of view of more than one character. Kevin Henkes uses this device effectively in *Bird Lake Moon*, which takes place over the course of a single summer. Henkes shows the developing friendship between Mitch and Spencer, and builds tension by alternating the points of view so that readers know both boys are keeping secrets from each other. Since it is a little more difficult for children to follow this kind of order, authors can make it easier, as Henkes did, by shifting the viewpoint between, rather than within, chapters and by using the characters' names as chapter headings so that young readers know from the outset which character is speaking.

More complex still is the use of *flashbacks* in which the author disrupts a linear chronology to recount events that occurred at an earlier time, usually to give readers insight into a character. This sort of narrative order can be very difficult for less experienced child readers to follow, as they expect events to happen in a chronological sequence and will struggle to fit the past events into the present. For them, the flashback needs to be clearly framed in some way so that they understand the shift in time. Sharon Creech accomplished this in *Walk Two Moons* by introducing the flashbacks as a series of brief episodes in a continuing story that thirteen-year-old Salamanca tells her grandparents on a cross-country car trip. With frequent interruptions from Sal's grandparents, young readers never lose sight of where they are in time; in a sense, the flashbacks seem to occur in the present, since they are part of a story being told in the present.

CONFLICT

Conflict is a major element of plot that keeps the story moving and stirs the interest of the reader who wants to find out what happens next and how the conflict will be resolved. Stories with little or no conflict are dull and slow moving, and inspire readers to say that nothing happened in the book. Conversely, stories with nothing but conflict seem shallow and contrived. Most formula series fiction, for example, is heavy on conflict, light on character.

To build a plot, an author places the main character (*protagonist*) into situations in which she comes into conflict with something or someone else (*antagonist*). The antagonist might be another character, nature, society, or self. A great many children's novels center on *character versus character* conflict, from the stories about facing up to the bully down the street to those about adjusting to life with a new stepparent. Stanley Yelnats and the other inmates at Camp Green Lake are pitted against the unsavory adult authority figures in Louis Sachar's *Holes*, and the conflict between the two groups drives the plot. *Character versus nature* has been popularized in survival stories, such as *The Young Man and the Sea*, by Rodman Philbrick, in which a twelve-year-old boy lost at sea struggles to survive and reels in a gigantic fish in the meantime. These two types of conflict are by far the most common in children's novels aimed at eight- to eleven-year-olds, most likely because they detail the type of outward struggles with which children can easily identify.

Character versus society need not involve conflict with society at large; instead it may be society in microcosm, viewed on a child's scale, such as the society of a neighborhood or school. Jerry Spinelli brilliantly uses this sort of conflict on a scale children can comprehend in *Wringer*, when ten-year-old Palmer refuses to participate in a cruel rite of passage. In children's novels, *character versus self* can be developed as an inner conflict a character faces, centered on moral dilemmas a child reader can easily grasp. For example, a homeless girl constantly questions her own actions when she steals a dog so she can claim the reward money in *How to Steal a Dog*, by Barbara O'Connor.

Plot Development

Conflict can be used in different ways to build different types of plots. An *episodic* plot is made up of a series of conflicts that are introduced and resolved, usually chapter by chapter. Episodic plots are generally easier for newly independent readers, who often have difficulty sustaining concentration when they first begin to read chapter books. Beverly Cleary's popular books about Henry Huggins, Beezus, and Ramona are perfect for this level, largely due to their episodic plots.

In a *progressive* plot, conflict is introduced early in the book and carried through until there is a climax and resolution near the story's end. Progressive plots generally follow the same general pattern of action:

1. Presentation of brief background that sets the stage
2. Introduction of conflict
3. Development of conflict
4. Climax or turning point
5. Resolution

In children's novels, the conflict is generally introduced very early in the book: Something happens to grab the reader's attention, to arouse curiosity, to entice the child to read on. After briefly setting the scene as Copenhagen in World War II, Lois Lowry introduces the conflict on page two of *Number the Stars*, when the main characters, racing each other home from school, are stopped by German soldiers.

The development of conflict is an essential part of the plot, since it accounts for most of a novel. It must be well paced so that the story doesn't lag, and it must continually stimulate the reader's interest. An author can achieve this by using two devices: *suspense* and *foreshadowing*.

Suspense raises questions into the reader's mind: What will happen next? Why did the character do that? When the girls come up against the German soldiers in *Number the Stars*, for example, we immediately wonder: Why would soldiers stop a group of little girls? Have they done something wrong? Are the soldiers friends or enemies? We keep reading to find out. Suspense that occurs at the end of a chapter is referred to as a *cliff-hanger*, and it propels readers directly into the next chapter so that they can find out what happens.

Foreshadowing gives us clues as to what will happen later in the story. To use the same example from *Number the Stars*, two instances of fore-shadowing occur in the scene with the soldiers. We note that one of the girls, Ellen, finds the experience much more frightening than her friend Annemarie does. We will later learn that Ellen is Jewish. Annemarie's little sister, Kirsti, on the other hand, pushes one soldier's hand away and says *"Don't!"* when he strokes her hair. This foreshadows the acts of resistance we will see later in the book. Foreshadowing builds anticipation, causing readers to make predictions about what will happen later in the story.

When foreshadowing is obvious and frequent, the plot is said to be predictable. In general, children seem far less troubled by predictable plots than adults. Many children express delight at figuring out a book's ending on their own—and then they'll turn around and read the whole thing over again, just to bask a while in their own cleverness.

A good example of less obvious foreshadowing was present in the opening scene from *Number the Stars*: Annemarie encounters German soldiers once again at the end of the book, and she survives by behaving as her little sister Kirsti did in the first encounter. Subtle uses of foreshadowing give readers a sense that the ending was inevitable, even if they did not guess the outcome. Experienced readers usually find this sort of ending more satisfying.

And what about that ending? After a steady buildup of suspense and foreshadowing, the protagonist ultimately engages in some sort of final confrontation with the antagonist, which will lead to a turning point in the conflict and a resolution. In children's novels, the protagonist almost always wins the battle against the antagonist. To return once again to *Number the Stars*, the final confrontation occurs when Annemarie carries a basket containing something of utmost importance to her uncle in the Resistance movement and she is stopped by German soldiers. By pretending to be a silly little girl carrying lunch to her uncle, she outwits the soldiers and manages to get the important information to her uncle so that he can help her friend Ellen escape to Sweden. Two chapters follow this climactic scene and give a final resolution to the story so that readers feel a sense of satisfaction and completeness. Occasionally, a children's novel will leave matters unresolved in an *open ending* by suggesting two or more possible interpretations and leaving it up to the reader to decide what happened. This was done most famously by Lowry in another of her books, *The Giver*.

Novels for children sometimes use more complex structures than a straightforward progressive or episodic plot. A *parallel* structure builds two progressive plots simultaneously. Louis Sachar skillfully developed two parallel plots in *Holes*, weaving an account of events from four generations earlier into the contemporary story of Stanley Yelnats, who was cursed due to the actions of his great-great-grandfather. Sachar makes an otherwise complex structure straightforward by clearly delineating time, place, and characters, so that readers know exactly where they are at every point in the story.

Another possible structure in children's fiction combines a progressive main plot with subplots. There are several subplots involving both people and animals that occur simultaneously to the two parallel plots in Kathi Appelt's *The Underneath*. The author uses short chapters, episodic chronological action, and a strong sense of place to tie them all together so that the story is easy for children to follow.

When you evaluate the plot of any children's novel, think of it from several angles. What kind of narrative order does it have? Will this order be clear for the intended audience? If the author chose a more complex type of order, what purpose does it serve? How does it illuminate character or advance the plot? What kind of conflict do you notice in the story? Is there too much or not enough conflict present? How is the conflict used to build the plot? What type of plot structure is used? Is it appropriate for the intended audience? If the plot structure is more complex, how does the author clarify the ordering of events for young readers? Do you notice clear instances of suspense and foreshadowing? How is conflict resolved in the story? Does the resolution seem credible?

CHARACTERIZATION

The *characters* are a crucial part of any children's novel, because they serve as a link between the reader and the story. The link is established when the child reader is able to identify with the actions, motives, and feelings of the main character in a story. One way for the author to accomplish this is to choose a main character who is close to the same age as readers in the book's target audience. A book aimed at nine- to eleven-year-olds, for instance, is less likely to succeed if its protagonist is only six years old. On the other hand, children do like to identify with characters who are a couple of years older than they are, so a book aimed at nine- to eleven-year-olds works well with a thirteen-year-old protagonist.

TYPES OF CHARACTERS

Authors can also establish identity between the protagonist and the reader by creating a main character who seems realistic and believable. Through *character development* the author reveals complexity by showing us how characters think, act, and feel, so that readers get a sense of a real, three-dimensional person. Not all characters in a story need to be equally as well developed in order for the novel to succeed as good fiction.

Secondary characters play smaller roles and often serve a different purpose, such as to advance the plot. They are usually defined by one or two characteristics alone and therefore seem to be one-dimensional or *flat*. Sometimes these characteristics are immediately recognizable because we've seen them countless times in other books and on television. Those created in this way are called *stock characters*. The pirate with an eye patch and a peg leg is one example of a stock character; and the smart, prissy girl who is the teacher's pet is another. When the characteristics have their basis in a recognized cultural or social shorthand, the stock characters are said to be *stereotyped*. We see this in such stock characters as the African-American kid who's good at basketball, or the Asian-American kid who's good at math. While an author might succeed in making a case for traits of this sort in a fully developed character, the use of them as defining characteristics for secondary characters is an indication of laziness—or even bias, conscious or otherwise—on the part of the author.

Primary characters are those who are closer to the central conflict in the story, and since they play a larger role, we expect a higher degree of character development. We refer to well-developed characters as *rounded* and those who grow and change over the course of a novel as *dynamic*. Since most children's novels feature child characters who experience some degree of maturation as a result of the conflict they face, we expect good fiction to have a dynamic, rounded main character.

CHARACTER DEVELOPMENT

We come to know characters in several different ways by observing how they look, what they do, what they think, what they say, and how they are viewed by other characters in the book. Throughout the course of a novel, an author reveals complexities of character through *appearance, action, thought*, and *dialogue*. A well-rounded character is developed using a combination of all these devices. I will cite some examples of how this is done, using the character D Foster in Jacqueline Woodson's *After Tupac & D Foster*.

Readers build mental images of characters based on what the author tells us about a character's *appearance*. As a surface quality, it is often the defining characteristic in a secondary character, but it is rarely definitive in a rounded, primary character. An author can use a description of appearance to arouse a reader's curiosity about a character initially, as Woodson does when the narrator gives us her first impression of D:

> She was tall and skinny and looked like she thought she was cute with her green eyes and pretty sort of half way of smiling at us. Her hair was in a bunch of braids with black rubber bands at the end of every single one. The braids were long, coming down over her shoulders and across her back, and her hair was this strange dark coppery color I'd never seen on a black girl—not naturally. She was wearing a T-shirt that said "HELLO MY NAME IS" in green letters, only there

wasn't a name after that, so it didn't make any sense whatsoever. I looked down at her feet. She had on white-girl clogs like you saw on the girls on TV—the ones with blond hair who lived in places like California or Miami or somewhere.

This description of D's appearance makes it clear that she is quite different from the narrator and her friend who've known each other all their lives. Like them, readers will want to know where D came from and who she is.

Actions are also visible only on the surface but they provide more insight into character because they spring from internal thoughts and motives. While many actions in a novel serve to move the plot along, some exist only to reveal character. Note, for example, what the following description of action tells us about D's character: *"D finished her other braid and looked at her watch—she'd bought it for ten dollars in Times Square, and most of the time it worked. She always wore it and was always checking it."* In just two sentences, we learn that D has some degree of independence—she has her own money and has bought something for herself in Times Square. But her actions also imply that someone, somewhere, expects her to be home at a certain time. Her independence has its limits.

The author can directly enter the main character's mind to reveal aspects of character through *thought*. In the passage quoted above about D's appearance, we get a good sense of the narrator's first impression of her through her thoughts, and this tells us as much about her as it does about D. Since Woodson uses the first person point of view of an unnamed narrator, she can't enter D's head, but she still is able to reveal some of D's thoughts through unconscious dialogue:

"I know it sounds whack," she said, so softly it sounded like she was talking to herself almost. "But when I see him on TV, I be thinking

154

about the way his life was all crazy. And we both all sad about it and stuff. But we ain't trying to let the sad feelings get us down. We ain't trying to give up."

The two friends are so stunned by D's sharing her innermost thoughts that they both stop talking, hoping D will say more. But she doesn't. That leads the narrator and Neeka to consider their own lives in contrast to D's, and to reveal more about all the characters through *dialogue*:

> *"Neeka," I said as we headed into my house. "You think we the lucky ones?"*
>
> *Neeka stopped at the bottom stair leading up to my apartment. It was warm in our hallway. Someone had baked something sweet and the smell made me hungry.*
>
> *"Like how?"*
>
> *I shrugged. "I don't know. When I heard D talking about her life like that . . . when she was saying about being hungry and—"*
>
> *"If we so lucky, how come she's the one get to take the bus all over the city* by herself *and don't have to worry about being home until nine o'clock?"*

With just a few lines of dialogue, Woodson shows us that the narrator is growing up a bit faster than her friend, as she is beginning to develop a more mature understanding of the world. Through the *comments of others*, an author can add further dimension to a character by showing us how she fits (or doesn't fit) into the social life surrounding her. Direct *comments of the author* can also be used for this purpose. Both must be used with care, or we end up with a less satisfying characterization that is based on telling, rather than showing, what a character is like.

All these factors must be taken into consideration when we evaluate characterization in fiction. What types of characters do you identify in the book? Are they realistic and believable? Is the main character dynamic? What devices does the author use to develop the main character? What kinds of changes do the characters undergo? How are secondary characters developed? What purposes do the secondary characters serve? How do events that occur in the novel shape the characters?

POINT OF VIEW

When authors create fictional worlds, they choose a particular stance within that world that defines what its perimeters will be. This is determined by *point of view*, the vantage point from which the action in the story is viewed and related. The author may choose to tell the story from inside a character's head or by looking over a character's shoulder or by viewing the entire scene from a distance. Each of these choices offers different advantages, challenges, and limitations.

First person point of view tells a story from inside the character's head. It is readily identifiable due to the use of the pronoun "I" by the narrator. First person has the advantage of evoking a powerful sense of reality through the immediacy of the character's voice. This strength is also its greatest limitation: The narrative is limited to what the main character thinks, observes, or hears from another character. Some authors try to get around this limitation by using dialogue in which one character briefs the protagonist to get information across to the reader. Overuse of this device may be an indication that the author has not mastered first person.

An **omniscient** point of view allows for much greater freedom and flexibility, in that the author can move around inside the story and enter the thoughts and feelings of any of the characters. The disadvantage is that it can make the story more difficult for young readers, as they often have difficulty following transitions from one character to the next. A *limited omniscient* point of view, in which the author uses third person but sticks to the viewpoint of one character, is easier for young readers to comprehend.

An **objective** point of view uses third person but does not enter the mind of a character at all. Rather, action is described completely by means of outside observations. This point of view is used effectively in realistic animal stories that dramatize action in the natural world. It becomes more challenging when used with human characters, because it requires readers to make their own connections between explicit actions and implicit emotions.

Children's authors sometimes bring together multiple points of view to construct a distinctive narrative. In *Bull Run*, Paul Fleischman used sixteen points of view to build a patchwork of history in a fictional account of the Civil War battle. In *Nothing But the Truth*, Avi employs dialogues, diary entries, memos, letters, and transcripts to build an unusual objective point of view from which readers must draw their own conclusions. In both these novels, the idea of point of view becomes the theme.

Whichever point of view an author chooses, he or she should remain consistent throughout. If he or she chooses to tell a story in the first person from the point of view of an eleven-year-old main character, he or she must stay with it. He or she cannot enter the mind of the character's mother or best friend or tell us things that the character hasn't experienced. When you evaluate point of view, keep the following questions in mind: Who is the narrator of the story, and what is this narrator likely to know?

SETTING

Setting in a novel can either function as a *backdrop* or as an *integral* part of the story. As the name suggests, backdrop settings are created from vivid descriptive details that may be interesting in and of themselves, but the story could easily be moved to another setting without losing much. Jack Gantos's popular series of books about Joey Pigza, for example, could be set in any contemporary American town. They draw their power from plot and characters, not from their setting.

Other novels would disintegrate if they were removed from their settings, because setting is integral to the action and characters. This is especially true of historical novels in which setting often functions to clarify the conflict in the story, as happens in Lois Lowry's *Number the Stars*. An integral setting must be clearly described and made as real as the characters so that the reader can not only picture it but feel it.

Aside from *clarifying conflict*, integral settings function in several ways. The setting can act as an *antagonist* as it invariably does in survival stories since the protagonist is always at the mercy of threats from the environment. In *Holes*, for example, the desert setting of Camp Green Lake makes day-to-day life difficult for Stanley, who must labor under the hot sun all day, digging holes. But it becomes even more antagonistic when he and Zero leave the camp and head out on their own into the barren wilderness.

Settings frequently serve to *illuminate character*. In her sequence of books about the Logan family, Mildred D. Taylor has created the fictional Depression-era small town, Strawberry, Mississippi, to explore race relations and to show the strength and dignity of the African-American family.

Setting can also operate on a *symbolic* level by encompassing two levels of meaning simultaneously. In *The Underneath*, setting functions in this way, as the "underneath" places are set in opposition to symbolize both safety and danger. This also extends to looking underneath the surface of a creature's skin to see deep inside its soul.

STYLE

Language dictates style in all writing. With respect to fiction, we look at both the literal and metaphorical ways an author uses language. What words has the author chosen and how have they been put together? *Literary devices* enrich the language of the novel and evoke emotional responses in the reader. Authors of children's fiction face a special challenge, as they write for an audience with limited experiences when it comes to understanding the symbolic use of language. Outstanding children's fiction uses literary devices geared directly toward young readers.

In *Words of Stone*, Kevin Henkes uses a remarkable range of literary devices, all based on a child's worldview. His prose is filled with *connotations* related to sensual childhood observations of people and the natural world of the backyard, making his metaphorical use of language easily understandable to child readers. I will use examples from *Words of Stone* to define the various types of literary devices.

Imagery is the use of words that appeal to any of the senses: sight, smell, sound, taste, and touch. *Words of Stone* is filled with child-friendly imagery: Blaze states that Joselle lives in "a house the color of celery." He notes that she "smelled dusty, like a ladybug" and he makes a reference to his own "blister-smooth skin."

Figurative language refers to the use of words in a nonliteral way. There are numerous examples of figurative language in *Words of Stone*, beginning with the title itself which signifies the difficulty Blaze has in communicating with his father, as well as Joselle's tendency to build walls between herself and others by lying. A common type of figurative language is *personification*, which means that nonhuman objects or animals are invested with human characteristics. Henkes uses personification when Blaze's father tosses a key across the breakfast table and it "stopped right beside Blaze's plate, kissing his fork." *Simile*, the comparison of two dissimilar things, generally with the words "like" or "as," is another common type of figurative language we see throughout the book. After Blaze spends a day playing outside, "dirt stuck to his body like bread crumbs," and when he speaks to Joselle, his voice is "as quiet as insect wings." *Metaphors* make implied comparisons. Henkes uses stones metaphorically throughout the novel on several different levels. These objects for serious outdoor play used by both Blaze and Joselle—by Blaze to mark the graves of his imaginary friends and by Joselle to spell out mean-spirited messages to Blaze—are linked by implication to the stone on Blaze's mother's grave. Once Blaze and Joselle resolve their differences, he observes, "the stones were white moons that bled together."

Hyperbole, the use of exaggeration, characterizes the speech of melodramatic Joselle: "For the first couple of years of your life, you were probably no bigger than a salt shaker. . . . I'll bet your parents have photographs from when you were three, but they tell you they were from the day you were born." By way of contrast, Blaze is often characterized with *understatement* to underscore his timid nature: "Blaze didn't particularly like spiders, except from a distance."

Kevin Henkes also uses *sound* devices to enrich the language of his novels. Some examples:

Alliteration: the repetition of initial consonants, as we see with both *s* and *l* in the phrase "legs scissoring the sunlight," which imitates the sound of scissors cutting.

Assonance: the repetition of similar vowel sounds. "Puddles dotted Floy's lawn like scattered mirrors." The long vowel sounds in the first four words come in quick succession like dripping water.

Consonance: the close repetition of consonant sounds. Note the repetition of the fluttering *l* sound when Joselle's grandmother tells her: "Your eyelids are the color of my needlepoint lilacs."

Onomatopoeia: the use of words that sound like their meanings.

We see an example of this when Blaze's father allows him to help attach canvas to frames. "The staple gun had a nasty little kick that jolted Blaze's arm, and it made a whooshing noise that reminded Blaze of getting a vaccination."

Rhythm: the pattern of words in a sentence, which gives it a particular flow, or *cadence*. Note the way Henkes uses rhythm in the following sentence to give readers a playful sense of somersaulting downhill: "Summer afternoons on the hill smelled of heat and dirt and grass and weeds and laziness."

Allusion makes reference to literature or historical events that are part of our common cultural heritage. It is less frequently used as a device in children's books simply because children typically do not have the necessary background to recognize and appreciate it. It is not, however, unheard of. Lois Lowry provides a stunning example of literary allusion in *Number the Stars* when Annemarie's courageous journey through the forest to take a basket of food to her uncle clearly echoes the story of "Little Red Riding Hood." Even though this is a folktale that most children know well, they might not expect it to show up in a novel. For this reason, Lowry draws a clear connection to it earlier in the novel with a scene in which Annemarie tells the story to her younger sister at bedtime.

Diction is another aspect of an author's style that enriches the manner in which a story is told. Sometimes referred to as the author's *voice*, diction injects prose with the flavor of a particular time and place by using words and grammatical structures native to the story's setting and characters. Diction can appear as distinctive in both dialogue and narrative. In dialogue, an author uses diction to approximate the way spoken language sounds. In narrative, diction creates a sense of the story as the characters who live in it might tell it themselves.

Christopher Paul Curtis is especially skilled at enlivening his novels with diction in both narrative and dialogue. Consider the following passage from *Bud, Not Buddy*, a novel set during the 1930s:

> *Billy'd stole a nickel from somewhere and held it up so's the buffalo on it was looking out at us. He pretended the buffalo was talking, it had a deep voice like you'd figure a buffalo would. It said, "Billy, my man, go ahead and bet this little no-momma fool that he don't know who his daddy is, then I'd have another nickel to bang around in your pocket with."*

Even in the narrative, Curtis's main character sounds as though he is speaking directly to the reader in his natural conversational style, and his dialogue gives us a sense of Billy's character. Compare this with the language he uses in another novel set in 1860, *Elijah of Buxton*:

> *"Elijah, you ain't gonna believe what Mr. Travis is fixing to teach us 'bout this morning!"*
> *I waren't gonna get myself worked up 'bout none of Mr. Travis's lessons. I ain't trying to say I'm smarter than Cooter, but I notice things a little better and carefuller than him, and Mr. Travis ain't showed no signs atall that he could come up with any lesson that was worth getting this excited over.*

Although both books use colloquial black English in the dialogue and the narrative, it's clear from the language that they are set in two different time periods.

Tone is the reflection of the author's attitude toward the story. It corresponds to the tone of voice in spoken language; however, since we can't hear a tone of voice in writing, the author conveys this sense through style. The tone in a children's novel may be humorous, as it is in *Elijah of Buxton*, or serious as it is in *After Tupac and D Foster*. In both these examples, the tone gives us an idea how the author feels about the story.

In children's books, we sometimes see instances of a condescending tone, which indicates that the author believes his or her ideas are really too complex for children to understand, so he or she must simplify it for them by explaining everything or trying to make it cute. We see, even more frequently, books with a sentimental tone. The latter often implies that the author believes all the world's great problems could be easily solved if they were viewed through the innocent eyes of a child. Other times a sentimental tone reveals that the author is fascinated by his own childhood but cares very little about the childhood of others, namely his readers.

To evaluate style, look at the ways in which an author uses language. Do you notice a distinctive style? How does the story sound when it is read aloud? What literary devices do you notice? How do these relate to the reality of child readers?

THEME

Theme is often one of the most elusive aspects of fiction, but it is an important one, because it answers the question: What is the story about? When you ask children this question, you often get a recitation of plot details in response. But theme is more than what happened in a story. Theme reflects the overall idea the author was trying to get across to readers in the first place. The fact that a child has difficulty articulating this deeper meaning doesn't necessarily mean that the theme wasn't understood.

All the pieces of a work of fiction—plot, characters, point of view, setting, and style—add up to its theme; that is, a significant truth that lies just beneath the surface of the story. If you, as an adult reader, have difficulty determining what, exactly, the theme of the book is, this may be an indication that the author did not have a clear theme in mind to start with or was unsuccessful in getting the idea across to readers through the story as it now stands. Conversely, many books are easily summed up in a phrase, which may suggest that the author did not succeed in combining fictional elements to give depth to the story.

When we examine theme in a work of children's fiction, it is important for us, as adults, to keep in mind that children are new to the idea of "significant truth." A truth that is commonplace to an experienced adult reader may be a real eye-opener for a child, particularly if the child is given the opportunity to discover meaning on his or her own. The thrill of discovery is the great promise a book holds for a reader.

In many outstanding works of fiction, the underlying truth, or theme, is left open to interpretation. The author sets the stage for discovery, but individual readers must be trusted to bring their own experiences to the reading of any book. When an author succeeds in writing a gripping story with a fresh style, peopled with characters who seem real and alive, her work is completed. The rest she leaves in the hands of the readers.

CHAPTER 8

Writing a Review

Children's book reviewing has had a long, rich history in the United States. In his landmark study, *The Rise of Children's Book Reviewing in America, 1865–1881*, Richard L. Darling found that children's books were regularly reviewed in mid- to late-nineteenth-century literary monthlies and popular magazines by reviewers who showed a considerable understanding of children and their books. More than one hundred years later, this sort of understanding continues to play a crucial role in children's book reviewing. Then, as now, the function of reviews appearing in the popular press was to call new books to the attention of potential readers, or, as Virginia Woolf succinctly described it: "partly to sort current literature; partly to advertise the author; partly to inform the public." This attention to new children's books in general periodical literature was carried well into the twentieth century with regular children's book review columns appearing in publications such as the *New York Herald Tribune*, *The New York Times Book Review*, the *Chicago Tribune*, and *The Saturday Review of Literature*.

With the development of children's library services in the early twentieth century, reviewing began to serve another function: to provide children's librarians with a guide for selecting books. *Booklist*, a professional library journal published by the American Library Association and consisting solely of reviews of new titles recommended for purchase, has included a children's books section since its inception in 1905. Other general library periodicals, such as *Kirkus Reviews* and *Library Journal*, included children's book reviews as well. *The Horn Book* magazine, founded in 1924 by Bertha Mahony Miller and Elinor Whitney Field, was entirely devoted to articles and reviews of children's books; and throughout much of the twentieth century it was very influential in setting contemporary standards for excellence in children's books. In 1954 the children's book section of *Library Journal* broke off to establish its own publication, *School Library Journal*, that strives to review every book published for children whether it is recommended for purchase or not. At the University of Chicago at Urbana-Champaign *The Bulletin of the Center for Children's Books* was established in 1945; it remains the only national journal to consist entirely of children's book reviews. Taken as a whole, these five journals (*Booklist*, *The Bulletin for the Center of Children's Books*, *The Horn Book*, *Kirkus Reviews*, and *School Library Journal*) comprise the basis for most school and public library book selection in the United States.

Many school and public library systems have created their own internal review processes that may require librarians to prepare written or oral reviews of newly published books being considered for purchase. Others use group discussion as a means of evaluating books and sharpening critical skills. With the rise of the internet, children's book reviewing has begun to take place online, often in blogs that are mostly or entirely devoted to providing reviews of new children's books. The quality of these reviews varies, but they cannot be entirely discounted; in fact, many of the blogs with children's book reviews have been created by librarians with professional training in book evaluation. Blogs offer the added advantage of immediacy and direct feedback from readers.

At the very least, children's librarians read a wide selection of reviews from the professional review journals listed above in order to make decisions about which books to purchase for the library collection. While some purchase decisions can be made quickly based on popular demand or professional wisdom, most selections are made with a great deal of care and deliberation, based, in whole or in part, on reviews. The reviewer, then, owes it to her audience to use care and deliberation in preparing a review.

THE DISTINCTION BETWEEN REVIEWING AND LITERARY CRITICISM

Although the words "review" and "criticism" are often used interchangeably, most experts differentiate between the two by pointing out that reviews are limited by time and space; that is, a review is published as close as possible to the publication date of the book under consideration and the reviewer is generally limited to a set number of words.

In an eloquent essay entitled "Out on a Limb with the Critics: Some Random Thoughts on the Present State of the Criticism of Children's Literature," Paul Heins, former editor of *The Horn Book*, drew the following distinction: "Reviewing . . . is only concerned with what is imminent in publishing, with what is being produced at the present time; and does its job well by selecting, classifying, and evaluating—evaluating for the time being. Criticism deals with literature in perspective and places a book in a larger context. . . ."

This is not to say that criticism should not enter into reviewing. In fact, Heins makes the point in the same article that it would be virtually impossible to keep criticism out of a review: "Any form of literary classification, comparison, or evaluation must also be considered a form of criticism."

PREPARING TO REVIEW

Because the reviewer does not have the advantage of time, it is to his or her advantage to have a broad knowledge of contemporary children's literature as a context for "selecting, classifying, and evaluating." A solid background in the literature also helps the reviewer put the book into a context so that he or she can answer the questions: Are there other books like this one? If so, how does it compare to them? What does it offer that is unique?

SELECTING BOOKS TO REVIEW

When you write reviews for a professional journal or as part of an internal review process, chances are you will not have a choice about which books you will review, since they will most likely be assigned to you. These assignments may be made in accordance with your own particular areas of interest or expertise; however, if you are given a book about which you simply cannot be objective, return it so that it can be assigned to another reviewer who can give it a fair review. Part of any book review editor's job is to match books with reviewers, and he or she will no doubt appreciate your honesty if you feel you are not the right reviewer for the book. Since objectivity is an important part of every reviewer's approach, it is best not to review books written by personal friends (or enemies) and to avoid reviewing books that give you a chance to air a complaint or grind an ax.

If you are reviewing for a general publication, such as your local newspaper, you may have the opportunity to choose the books you will review. There are no hard-and-fast rules about what to select, but it is best to choose a book that is current, readily available, and likely to be of interest to the audience for whom you are writing. It may be the latest book by a well-known popular writer or a first book from a promising newcomer. You may choose a book to fit the current season (a great new biography about Abraham Lincoln for Presidents' Day, for example), a book that can be linked to a current news event, or one that you know will be of local interest. When you can articulate exactly why you have chosen to review one particular book over all the others at this particular time, you have already begun to write an opening sentence that will link the book to your audience.

READING AND NOTE TAKING

A reviewer's first obligation is to give a book a thorough and careful reading. There are, of course, different ways to approach this task. In her study of children's book reviewers, Kathleen W. Craver found that some reviewers prefer to read a book all the way through, jotting down an occasional note along the way, and then return for a second reading to make more detailed notes. Others take careful notes during their initial reading and read straight through the second time around to get a better sense of the author's style and pacing.

Before you begin to read, try to place the book in its broad category by type or genre: Is it nonfiction, a folktale, a transitional book? Usually (but not always) the classification is fairly straightforward. Once you have determined the category, you can use the corresponding chapter in *From Cover to Cover* as your framework for evaluation. As you read, you can jot down notes to outline the book's structure or the main developments in the plot; to respond to questions you ask yourself as part of the critical process; and to keep track of questions the book under review raises in your mind. These questions may require you to consult outside sources before you begin to write a review.

According to Craver's study, some reviewers write their review immediately after the second reading and some take up to a week to mull things over before beginning to write. Regardless of their approach, all the reviewers cited rereading and note taking as an essential part of the review process.

CONSULTING OUTSIDE SOURCES

Many of the reviewers who took part in Craver's study also indicated that they frequently sought outside information to assist them with a review. This generally consisted of discussing the book with a colleague or reading it aloud to a group of children to get their responses. It is not considered cheating to ask others for their opinions of a book you are reviewing. In fact, if you have kept an open mind toward the book, the responses of others can greatly enrich your critical perspective.

Many critics find it especially helpful to get responses from actual children. If there is an easy and natural way for you to do this, such as sharing a picture book with preschoolers during a regular library story time, by all means take advantage of the opportunity. But use the experience as one aspect of your critical approach, not the be-all and end-all of your assessment. And, please, never allow your review to sink into a description of your three-year-old daughter's response to the book. Because your relationship with the child is of a personal, rather than professional, nature, this is not only irrelevant and unprofessional, it is self-indulgent. Save it for your annual holiday form letter.

In the course of your note taking, if you jotted down any questions that require some outside fact-checking, this is the time to do it. When you are reviewing a nonfiction book, you may want to consult other books on the same subject for comparison. This will broaden your own background knowledge of the subject itself, and it will help you think about the book you are reviewing in contrast to other books for children on the same subject. You can mention related children's books in your review to compare and contrast the new book to others that are available. Librarians, in particular, appreciate these sorts of critical insights; however, it is important that you don't allow yourself to get carried away. Your primary responsibility is to review one book, not to write about every book that has been published to date on the same subject.

We have all had the experience of reading a work of fiction in which certain historical, regional, or cultural details just don't ring true. This can raise questions such as: Would it have been likely for a nineteenth-century Amish family to join a wagon train? Did the Iroquois live in tipis? Is the black English an author uses in dialogue accurate? You may want to follow up on some of these questions, especially if it is an essential part of the book. Using the question about the Amish family as an example: If the family itself is the central focus of the book and their joining the wagon train a major factor in the plot, it would be important for you to do some background research to answer the question. If they are merely mentioned briefly in one paragraph in chapter 4, you may not want to spend a lot of time pursuing it.

Occasionally, reviewers seek the opinions of content specialists to help determine the accuracy or authenticity of a book that raises questions. If you suspect there is a problem with a book that claims one can avoid contracting HIV by showering after unprotected sex, for example, you can double-check the facts with a local expert to confirm your suspicions. If you do consult a content specialist, remember that while a content specialist is an expert in his or her particular field and is able to evaluate the accuracy of *what* information is provided, you are the expert when it comes to *how* this information is presented in a book for children.

WHAT TO INCLUDE IN A BIBLIOGRAPHIC CITATION

All reviews must open with a bibliographic citation that includes details such as author, title, and publisher. Although reviewers have many choices to make concerning the content of their reviews, bibliographic citations are fairly standard.

Reviews that are published in general publications such as newspapers and popular magazines, typically include only a brief heading that includes title (including subtitle), author, illustrator (if any), publisher, price, and sometimes the year of publication and number of pages. Every publication has its own in-house style for citations. You will need to include a complete citation at the head of your review. A standard style for citations appearing in general publication is:

The London Eye Mystery. By Siobhan Dowd. David Fickling Books/Random House, 2008. 322 pages. $15.99

For an illustrated book:

The Graveyard Book. By Neil Gaiman. Illustrated by Dave McKean. HarperCollins, 2008. 320 pages. $17.99

Since reviews that appear in professional review journals are used for book selection, the bibliographic citations are more detailed and always include the International Standard Book Number (ISBN) for both the trade and library binding. In addition, they also may include the Library of Congress (LC) number, publication date, and an indication as to whether the book was reviewed from galleys. The reviews themselves are generally arranged by the last name of the author, and that information appears first in bibliographic citations in review journals. Every journal's style for citing bibliographic information varies slightly but, for the most part, they contain the same information:

Dowd, Siobhan. *The London Eye Mystery*. David Fickling Books/Random House, 2008. 322 pages. Tr. $15.99, ISBN 978-0-375-84976-3; PLB $18.99, ISBN 978-0-375-94976-0

For an illustrated book:

Gaiman, Neil. *The Graveyard Book*. Illustrated by Dave McKean. HarperCollins, 2008. 320 pages. Tr. $17.99, 978-0-06-053092-1; PLB $18.89, 978-0-06-053093-8

WRITING THE REVIEW

Once you have done all the necessary reading, note taking, and fact-checking, you are ready to begin writing the actual review. A good review will briefly describe the contents, scope, and style of a book; critically assess its quality; and suggest its potential audience. Phyllis K. Kennemer has labeled these categories: descriptive, analytical, and sociological. She gives the following examples to illustrate:

Descriptive: Objective statements about the characters, plot, theme, or illustrations.

Analytical: Statements about literary and artistic elements, including evaluation, comparison, and mention of contributions to the field.

Sociological: Judgments based on nonliterary considerations, such as potential controversial elements or predictions about popularity.

One of the most common criticisms of children's book reviews today is that they rely heavily on description and include very little in the way of analysis.

As you begin to sketch out your review, it may be helpful to think about your responses in terms of these categories, as you will want to include each type of statement in your review. As a way of getting started, divide a piece of scratch paper into three sections and label them "descriptive," "analytical," and "sociological." Using your notes, make a list of all the points you would like to include in your review, placing each one in its corresponding category. If the descriptive side of your paper seems to be filling up rapidly and there is very little in the analytical or sociological category to balance it, try using the descriptive points listed as a springboard for critical thinking by asking yourself questions about them. If you have noted, for example, that the book is illustrated with color photographs, ask yourself how they support the text. Are they well placed? Do they have clear captions? What sorts of things do they show?

DECIDING WHAT TO INCLUDE

Because reviews are generally brief (100 to 400 words, with the average length of 150 words in children's book review journals), you will obviously not be able to include all your points, so you will have to decide which ones are the most important. Consider these questions: Which points relate to the book as a whole? Which ones will give readers a sense of the book's style or unique qualities? Which ones best support your overall objective assessment of the book? How do they contribute to a fair, balanced judgment about the book?

Children's book reviewers are sometimes taken to task by readers

174

who order a book based on positive reviews, only to find that one of the characters uses profanity on page 43. "Why didn't you mention that in the review?" the readers ask, accusing the reviewer of misleading them. Former book review editor Betsy Hearne discusses this issue at length her essay "A Reviewer's Story," concluding that as a reviewer, she opts to mention potentially controversial elements "only if they warrant analysis as an important aspect of the work. Anything more would serve as a censor signal to steer librarians away from dangerous books and focus attention on didactic evaluation."

Critic Zena Sutherland discussed the choices a reviewer must make when it comes to pointing out minor errors and discrepancies: "In a review, a negative comment can loom deceptively large and mislead the reader. If, for example, [a] pictorial discrepancy is minor, one doesn't want readers to assume that the illustrations are replete with careless details." Again, as Hearne stresses above, the mention of such details must be weighed against their significance to the book as a whole.

As you make decisions about what points to include in your review, you can also begin to think about how you will organize them. How do they relate to each other? Is there a logical order that emerges as you look at them together? Does one important element stand out as a central point in your evaluation? Can it be used as a thesis statement to open your review? Or will you start with a descriptive statement and then move on to your analytical points?

WRITING IT ALL DOWN

The opening sentence is important because it sets the tone for your entire review. Chosen with care, it can enliven your review and give it a logical structure that makes it easier for you to write and for others to read.

If you are writing for a general audience, you need to grab your readers' attention with the opening sentence. You may also need to provide a bit of context for them, since you can't assume that they know anything at all about children's books. Finding a hook that quickly links your audience to children's literature in general and the book you're reviewing specifically is an effective way to open a review for general readers:

> *With his popular, innovative books such as* The Way Things Work *(Houghton, 1988) and the Caldecott Award–winner* Black and White *(Houghton, 1990), David Macaulay has established himself as a master at producing books in which words and pictures work together to create a story that must be completed in the reader's imagination.*

When I wrote this opening sentence in a review of David Macaulay's *Shortcut* for the Milwaukee *Journal Sentinel*, I consciously used a reference to the Caldecott Medal because I assumed that most adult readers would recognize it as significant, even if they had never heard of David Macaulay. I also used the adjectives "popular" and "innovative" to describe his books not only because they are appropriate but because I thought they would be likely to pique a general reader's interest. I wanted to make the casual reader stop and think: "Hmmm, what sort of books are popular with kids today? What is considered innovative?"

One of the first things readers see when they look at a review is the title of the book. You may want to open a review by making some reference to the title, particularly if it is intriguingly unusual.

Deborah Stevenson does this effectively in her review of Jeremy Tankard's *Me Hungry!*:

> *Pre-dinner appetite apparently really is an age-old dilemma, since in this case it's plaguing Edwin, a Stone Age kid, whose com-*

plaint of "Me hungry!" is received by Father and Mother in turn
with a resounding "Me busy!"

Stevenson manages to explain the book's premise and odd title in just one sentence that also tells us when the book is set, who the main character is, and that the story is comical.

The majority of reviews in professional journals begin with a descriptive account of the book itself. These need not be dry summations, however. Notice how effectively Roger Sutton describes the plot of Alexandra Day's picture book *Carl's Summer Vacation*:

> *Up at the family's cabin, Rottweiler Carl and his charge Madeleine*
> *are supposed to be taking a nap, but, as usual, no. The two go*
> *canoeing (after Carl thoughtfully puts the toddler into a life jacket),*
> *gleefully fall into the water, visit a playground, interrupt a ball*
> *game, and surreptitiously feast on somebody else's picnic.*

Sutton's opening sentence works both for those familiar with the series and characters, and those who are not, by implying that these two are accustomed to trouble, and his list of what they get into suggests fast-paced action, as well as the characters' attitude toward events.

Another technique for an opening is to launch right into a critical analysis and then go on to use descriptive statements as examples. This is how Ilene Cooper approaches Rebecca and Ed Emberley's retelling of *Chicken Little*:

> *You think you know the story of Chicken Little? Well, maybe you*
> *do, but the Emberleys' hip, happening illustrations will make you*
> *see it in a whole new way. As before, Chicken Little ("not the*
> *brightest chicken in the coop") gets hit with an acorn and assumes*

the sky is falling. Soon the usual suspects—Loosey Goosey, Turkey Lurkey, et al.—are given the news with much squawking and shaking.

Note that Cooper's words do double duty, providing description and analysis simultaneously. Her prose style also echoes the playful nature of the retelling to give readers a clear sense of the book's essence, and her tone shows that she expects the readers to know the story so they can appreciate the humor of the Emberleys' interpretation.

No matter what sort of opening you use, your review should include a mix of descriptive and analytical statements so that readers will know what the book is about and what you thought of it. It should be clear to them whether you recommend the book or not. Do not be afraid to express your opinion, as long as you can back it up with evidence from the book.

Many readers, particularly librarians and teachers, appreciate comments about a book's popular appeal or suggestions of how it might be shared with children. They like to know if a novel would make a good classroom read aloud for fourth graders or if a picture book would work well in a toddler story hour. Be as specific as possible. Comments such as "Will appeal to everyone" are meaningless while those such as "Will appeal to Lemony Snicket fans" tell readers something definite about the subject, scope, and reading level. Of course, you don't have to make predictions about a book's appeal, and it is better to say nothing at all than to make vague or inaccurate guesses.

In all professional journals and in many popular publications, reviewers are expected to indicate an age range for the book's target audience. This judgment should be based on your own knowledge of children's responses to literature and your assessment of the book itself, not the ages suggested by the publisher.

Once you have the first rough draft down on paper, read it over critically. Is there too much description? Not enough? Did you forget to mention something important? Do you notice anything in it that is clever for its own sake? Or is the review simply too long?

Take a look at how your sentences are structured. Can any of them be condensed and combined? Look for any forms of the verb "to be"—a weak verb (unless you're Shakespeare). If you can replace it with a strong one, you will improve your review by saying the same thing in fewer words. For example:

"Amelia is an independent girl who wants to be an airline pilot when she grows up."

can be changed to:

"Independent Amelia plans to fly planes one day."

Look for redundancies. Have you said the same thing in two different ways? In the above example, I was able to delete the word "girl" because the character's personal name makes her gender clear. When you are reviewing a nonfiction book, its title often specifies content that you do not need to repeat. Marfé Ferguson Delano's *Helen's Eyes: A Photobiography of Annie Sullivan, Helen Keller's Teacher* provides a good example.

If you feel that your writing is perfect and the review is still too long, you are simply going to have to cut out a sentence or two. Read the review over one more time to find the lines that can be deleted without losing an important point or aspect. The skill with which Deborah Stevenson, Roger Sutton, and Ilene Cooper write reviews comes from their years of experience as professional reviewers and writers. Each one writes with a distinctive style that owes its liveliness to a use of clear, simple English. As a novice reviewer, you may find it helpful to read and analyze their reviews (and those of other professional reviewers), thinking critically about how they structure them and noting the verbs and adjectives they use. With practice, experience, and perseverance, you will sharpen your own skills.

The critic John Rowe Townsend says, "Good reviewers of children's books are probably scarcer than good writers of them. And it is almost as necessary that there should be good and effective writing about children's books as that there should be good children's books. Conceivably, indeed, it is necessary in order that there should continue to *be* good children's books."

Welcome.

Source Notes and Bibliography

Brackets around page numbers indicate that the book did not include printed page numbers.

CHAPTER 1: A CRITICAL APPROACH TO CHILDREN'S BOOKS

CITATIONS

Phillip Hoose quote p. 17 from *The Race to Save the Lord God Bird*, p. 186.

Susan Campbell Bartoletti quote p. 19 from *Hitler Youth*, p. 162.

SOURCES

Aronson, Marc. "Do Books Still Matter?" *School Library Journal* 53:4 (April 2007), pp. 36–39.

Briley, Dorothy. "The Impact of Reviewing on Children's Book Publishing," in *Evaluating Children's Books: A Critical Look*, edited by Betsy Hearne and Roger Sutton. Urbana-Champaign, IL: University of Illinois, 1993, pp. 105–17.

Dessauer, John P. *Book Publishing: The Basic Introduction*. New expanded ed. New York: Continuum, 1989.

Dresang, Eliza T. *Radical Change: Books for Youth in a Digital Age.* New York: H. W. Wilson, 1999.

Giblin, James Cross. *Writing Books for Young People.* New ed. Boston: The Writer, 1998.

Heppermann, Christine. "Reading in the Virtual Forest," *The Horn Book* 76:6 (November/December 2000), pp. 687–92.

Karl, Jean E. *How to Write and Sell Children's Picture Books.* Cincinnati, OH: Writer's Digest Books, 1994.

Litowinsky, Olga. *It's a Bunny-Eat-Bunny World: A Writer's Guide to Surviving and Thriving in Today's Competitive Children's Book Market.* New York: Walker, 2001.

———. *Writing and Publishing Books for Children in the 1990s: The Inside Story from the Editor's Desk.* New York: Walker, 1992.

Marcus, Leonard S. *Minders of Make-Believe: Idealists, Entrepreneurs, and the Shaping of American Children's Literature.* Boston: Houghton Mifflin, 2008.

McElderry, Margaret K. "Remarkable Women: Anne Carroll Moore & Company," *School Library Journal* 38:3 (March, 1992), pp. 156–62.

McNamara, Shelley G. "Early Public Library Work with Children," *Top of the News* 43:1 (Fall 1986), pp. 59–72.

Rosen, Judith. "Taking Steps into the Digital Future," *Publishers Weekly* 256 (February 16, 2009), pp. 17–19.

CHILDREN'S BOOK CITED

Bartoletti, Susan Campbell. *Hitler Youth: Growing Up in Hitler's Shadow.* New York: Scholastic, 2005.

Harris, Robie H. *It's NOT the Stork! A Book about Girls, Boys, Babies, Bodies, Families, and Friends.* Illustrated by Michael Emberley. Cambridge, MA: Candlewick, 2006.

Hoose, Phillip. *The Race to Save the Lord God Bird*. New York: Melanie Kroupa Books/Farrar, Straus, and Giroux, 2004.

Raven, Margot Theis. *Let Them Play*. Illustrated by Chris Ellison. Chelsea, MI: Sleeping Bear, 2005.

CHAPTER 2: BOOKS OF INFORMATION

CITATIONS

Jean Fritz quote p. 25 from "Biography: Readability and Responsibility," p. 759.

Laurence Pringle quote p. 39 from: *Alligators and Crocodiles!*, p. [1].

Kadir Nelson quote p. 40 from *We Are the Ship*, p. 2.

Sid Fleischman quote p. 41 from *The Trouble Begins at 8*, p. 87.

Sally M. Walker quote pp. 41–42 from *Secrets of a Civil War Submarine*, p. 89.

Milton Meltzer quote p. 42 from "Beyond Fact," p. 30.

Walter Dean Myers quote pp. 42–43 from *Now Is Your Time!*, p. 71.

Tanya Lee Stone quote p. 43 from *Almost Astronauts*, p. 87.

Jim Murphy quote p. 46 from *An American Plague*, p. 142.

SOURCES

Broadway, Marsha D., and Malia Howland. "Science Books for Young People: Who Writes Them?" *School Library Journal* 37:5 (May 1991), pp. 35–38.

Carter, Betty. "Reviewing Nonfiction for Children: Stance, Scholarship and Structure," in *Evaluating Children's Books: A Critical Look*, edited by Betsy Hearne and Roger Sutton. Urbana-Champaign, IL: University of Illinois, 1993, pp. 59–71.

Carter, Betty, and Richard F. Abrahamson. *Nonfiction for Young Adults:*

From Delight to Wisdom. Phoenix, AZ: Oryx, 1990.

Epstein, Connie C. "Accuracy in Nonfiction," *School Library Journal* 33:7 (March 1987), pp. 113–15.

Faust, Susan. "In Quest of Excellence: The Sibert Committee Looks at 14 Qualities of a Truly Distinguished Information Book," *School Library Journal* 47:6 (June 2001), pp. 42–43.

Freedman, Russell. "On Telling the Truth," *Booklist* 95:2 (September 15, 1998), pp. 224–25.

Fritz, Jean. "Biography: Readability and Responsibility," *The Horn Book* 64:6 (November/December 1988), pp. 759–60.

Giblin, James Cross. "More Than Just Facts: A Hundred Years of Children's Nonfiction," *The Horn Book* 76:4 (July/August 2000), pp. 413–24.

———. "The Rise and Fall and Rise of Juvenile Nonfiction, 1961–1988," *School Library Journal* 35:2 (October 1988), pp. 27–31.

Hunt, Jonathan. "Where Do All the Prizes Go?: Thoughts on the State of Informational Books," *The Horn Book* 81:4 (July/August 2005), pp. 439–45.

Isaacs, Kathleen. "Truth in Information Books," *School Library Journal* 51:7 (July 2005), pp. 28–29.

Meltzer, Milton. "Beyond Fact," in *Beyond Fact: Nonfiction for Children and Young People*. Edited by Jo Carr. Chicago: American Library Association, 1982.

———. "Where Do All the Prizes Go? The Case for Nonfiction," *The Horn Book* 52:1 (February 1976), pp. 17–23.

Millhouser, Frances. "Beautiful Science: Books That Cash in on Children's Curiosity," *School Library Journal* 37:5 (May 1991), pp. 47–48.

Wilson, Sandip. "Getting Down to Facts in Children's Nonfiction Literature: A Case for the Importance of Sources," *Journal of Children's Literature* 32:1 (Spring 2006), pp. 56–63.

Bishop, Nic. *Spiders*. New York: Scholastic, 2007.

Blumberg, Rhoda. *Commodore Perry in the Land of the Shogun*. New York: Lothrop, Lee & Shepard, 1985.

Burns, Loree Griffin. *Tracking Trash: Flotsam, Jetsam, and the Science of Ocean Motion*. Boston: Houghton Mifflin, 2007.

Cole, Joanna. *The Magic School Bus Lost in the Solar System*. Illustrated by Bruce Degen. New York: Scholastic, 1990.

Cowley, Joy. *Red-Eyed Tree Frog*. Photographs by Nic Bishop. New York: Scholastic, 1999.

Crosby, Jeff, and Shelley Ann Jackson. *Little Lions, Bull Baiters & Hunting Hounds: A History of Dog Breeds*. Plattsburgh, NY: Tundra, 2008.

Fleischman, Sid. *Escape! The Story of the Great Houdini*. New York: Greenwillow Books, 2006.

———. *The Trouble Begins at 8: A Life of Mark Twain in the Wild, Wild West*. New York: Greenwillow Books, 2008.

Fleming, Candace. *The Lincolns: A Scrapbook Look at Abraham and Mary*. New York: Schwartz & Wade Books/Random House, 2008.

Freedman, Russell. *Lincoln: A Photobiography*. New York: Clarion Books, 1987.

———. *Who Was First? Discovering the Americas*. New York: Clarion Books, 2007.

Gerstein, Mordicai. *The Man Who Walked Between the Towers*. Brookfield, CT: Roaring Brook, 2003.

Gibbons, Gail. *My Baseball Book*. New York: HarperCollins, 2000.

———. *My Basketball Book*. New York: HarperCollins, 2000.

———. *My Football Book*. New York: HarperCollins, 2000.

———. *My Soccer Book*. New York: HarperCollins, 2000.

Jackson, Ellen. *The Mysterious Universe: Supernovae, Dark Energy, and Black Holes*. Photographs and illustrations by Nic Bishop. Boston:

Houghton Mifflin, 2008.

Jenkins, Steve, and Robin Page. *Sisters & Brothers: Sibling Relationships in the Animal World*. Boston: Houghton Mifflin, 2008.

Krensky, Stephen. *Comic Book Century: The History of American Comic Books*. Minneapolis: Twenty-First Century Books, 2008.

Kuklin, Susan. *Families*. New York: Hyperion, 2006.

Lasky, Kathryn. *Sugaring Time*. Photographs by Christopher G. Knight. New York: Macmillan, 1983.

Lauber, Patricia. *Volcano: The Eruption and Healing of Mount St. Helen's*. New York: Bradbury, 1986.

Levine, Karen. *Hana's Suitcase: A True Story*. Morton Grove, IL: Albert Whitman, 2003.

Lutes, Jason, and Nick Bertozzi. *Houdini: The Handcuff King*. New York: Hyperion, 2007.

Madden, Kerry. *Harper Lee: Up Close*. New York: Viking Children's Books, 2009.

Martin, Jacqueline Briggs. *Snowflake Bentley*. Illustrated by Mary Azarian. Boston: Houghton Mifflin, 1998.

Meltzer, Milton. *Never to Forget: The Jews of the Holocaust*. New York: Harper & Row, 1976.

Murphy, Jim. *An American Plague: The True and Terrifying Story of the Yellow Fever Epidemic of 1793*. New York: Clarion Books, 2003.

Myers, Walter Dean. *Now Is Your Time!: The African-American Struggle for Freedom*. New York: HarperCollins, 1991.

Nelson, Kadir. *We Are the Ship: The Story of Negro League Baseball*. New York: Jump at the Sun/Hyperion, 2008.

Nelson, Scott Reynolds, with Marc Aronson. *Ain't Nothing but a Man: My Quest to Find the Real John Henry*. Washington, D.C.: National Geographic, 2008.

Pringle, Laurence. *Alligators and Crocodiles!: Strange and Wonderful*.

Illustrated by Meryl Henderson. Honesdale, PA: Boyds Mills, 2009.

Sattler, Helen Roney. *Hominids: A Look Back at Our Ancestors*. Illustrated by Christopher Santoro. New York: Lothrop, Lee & Shepard Books, 1988.

Siegel, Siena Cherson. *To Dance: A Memoir*. Illustrated by Mark Siegel. New York: Aladdin/Simon & Schuster, 2006.

Simon, Seymour. *Destination: Jupiter*. New York: William Morrow, 1998.

St. George, Judith. *So You Want to Be President?* Illustrated by David Small. New York: Philomel Books, 2000.

Stone, Tanya Lee. *Almost Astronauts: 13 Women Who Dared to Dream*. Somerville, MA: Candlewick, 2009

Thimmesh, Catherine. *Lucy Long Ago: Uncovering the Mystery of Where We Came From*. Boston: Houghton Mifflin Harcourt, 2009.

Thomas, Shelley Moore. *A Baby's Coming to Your House!* Photographs by Eric Futran. Morton Grove, IL: Albert Whitman, 2001.

Turner, Pamela S. *Life on Earth—and Beyond: An Astrobiologist's Quest*. Watertown, MA: Charlesbridge, 2008.

Walker, Sally M. *Secrets of a Civil War Submarine: Solving the Mysteries of the H. L. Hunley*. Minneapolis: Carolrhoda Books, 2005.

———. *Written in Bone: Buried Lives of Jamestown and Colonial Maryland*. Minneapolis: Carolrhoda Books, 2009.

Winick, Judd. *Pedro and Me: Friendship, Loss, and What I Learned*. New York: Henry Holt, 2000.

CHAPTER 3: TRADITIONAL LITERATURE

CITATIONS

Betsy Hearne quote p. 54 from "Cite the Source: Reducing Cultural Chaos in Picture Books, Part One," p. 27.

Betsy Hearne quote p. 54 from "Swapping Tales and Stealing Stories: The

Ethics and Aesthetics of Folklore in Children's Literature," p. 512.

Kevin Crossley-Holland quote p. 55 from *British Folk Tales: New Version*, p. 374.

Margaret Willey quote p. 57 from *The 3 Bears and Goldilocks*, p. [11].

Julius Lester quote p. 58 from *John Henry*, p. [12].

Margaret Read MacDonald quote pp. 58–59 from *Mabela the Clever*, p. [20].

John Bierhorst quote p. 59 from *The White Deer, and Other Stories Told from the Lenape*, p. 21.

Joseph Bruchac quote p. 60 from *The Girl Who Married the Moon*, p. 29.

Julie Cummins quote p. 66 from "Fractured Fairy Tales: Spin-Offs, Spoofs, and Satires," p. 51.

SOURCES

Cipielewski, James F. "What Tales Do We Tell of the Twentieth Century? Folktales and Fairy Tales Prosper," in *Children's Literature Remembered: Issues, Trends, and Favorite Books*. Edited by Linda M. Pavonetti. Westport, CT: Libraries Unlimited, 2004, pp. 49–64.

Cummins, Julie. "Fractured Fairy Tales: Spin-Offs, Spoofs, and Satires," *School Library Journal* 43:10 (October 1997), pp. 50–51.

Hearne, Betsy. "Cite the Source: Reducing Cultural Chaos in Picture Books, Part One," *School Library Journal* 39:7 (July 1993), pp. 22–27.

———. "Respect the Source: Reducing Cultural Chaos in Picture Books, Part Two," *School Library Journal* 39:8 (August 1993), pp. 33–37.

———. "Swapping Tales and Stealing Stories: The Ethics and Aesthetics of Folklore in Children's Literature," *Library Trends* 47:3 (Winter 1999), pp. 509–28.

Hepler, Susan. "Fooling Around with Folktales," *School Library Journal* 53:6 (June 2007), pp. 55–59.

Miller-Lachmann, Lyn. "Multicultural Publishing: The Folktale Flood," *School Library Journal* 40:2 (February 1994), pp. 35–36.

Opie, Iona, and Peter Opie. *The Classic Fairy Tales.* New York: Oxford University Press, 1974.

Reese, Debbie. "Proceed with Caution: Using Native American Folktales in the Classroom," *Language Arts* 84:3 (January 2007), pp. 245–56.

Stevenson, Deborah. "'If You Read This Last Sentence, It Won't Tell You Anything': Postmodernism, Self-Referentiality, and *The Stinky Cheese Man," Children's Literature Association Quarterly* 19:1 (Spring 1994), pp. 32–34.

Thurber, James. "Fables for Our Time—1," *The New Yorker* 14:49 (January 21, 1939), p. 19.

Yeh, Phoebe. "Multicultural Publishing: The Best and the Worst of Times," *Journal of Youth Services in Libraries* 6:2 (Winter 1993), pp. 157–60.

Yolen, Jane. "Once upon a While Ago: Folktales in the Course of Literature," in *Children's Literature Remembered: Issues, Trends, and Favorite Books.* Edited by Linda M. Pavonetti. Westport, CT: Libraries Unlimited, 2004, pp. 39–48.

CHILDREN'S BOOKS CITED

Barton, Byron. *The Three Bears.* New York: HarperCollins, 1991.

Bierhorst, John, ed. *The White Deer, and Other Stories Told by the Lenape.* New York: William Morrow, 1995.

Bruchac, Joseph, and Gayle Ross. *The Girl Who Married the Moon: Tales from Native North America.* Mahwah, NJ: BridgeWater Books, 1994.

Crossley-Holland, Kevin. *British Folk Tales: New Versions.* New York: Orchard Books, 1987.

Grimm, Jakob, and Wilhelm Grimm. *Hansel and Gretel.* Translated from the German by Elizabeth D. Crawford. Illustrated by Lisbeth Zwerger. New York: William Morrow, 1979.

————. *Hansel and Gretel*. Translated by Mrs. Edgar Lucas. Illustrated by Susan Jeffers. New York: Dial, 1980.

————. *Hansel and Gretel*. Adapted from the translation by Eleanor Quarrie. Illustrated by Anthony Browne. New York: Franklin Watts, 1981.

————. *Hansel and Gretel*. Translated and retold by Rika Lesser. Illustrated by Paul O. Zelinsky. New York: Dodd, Mead, 1984.

Kajikawa, Kimiko. *Tsunami!* Illustrated by Ed Young. New York: Philomel Books, 2009.

Lester, Julius. *John Henry*. Illustrated by Jerry Pinkney. New York: Dial Books, 1994.

MacDonald, Margaret Read. *Mabela the Clever*. Illustrated by Tim Coffey. Morton Grove, IL: Albert Whitman, 2001.

Marshall, James. *Goldilocks and the Three Bears*. New York: Dial Books, 1988.

Oberman, Sheldon. *Solomon and the Ant, and other Jewish Folktales*. Introduction and commentary by Peninnah Schram. Honesdale, PA: Boyds Mills, 2006.

Schwartz, Alvin. *In a Dark, Dark Room, and Other Scary Stories*. Illustrated by Dirk Zimmer. An I Can Read Book. New York: HarperCollins, 1984.

————. *Scary Stories to Tell in the Dark: Collected from American Folklore*. Illustrated by Stephen Gammell. New York: Lippincott, 1981.

Scieszka, Jon. *The True Story of the 3 Little Pigs, by A. Wolf.* Illustrated by Lane Smith. New York: Viking, 1989.

Wiesner, David. *The Three Pigs*. New York: Clarion Books, 2001.

Willey, Margaret. *The 3 Bears and Goldilocks*. Illustrated by Heather M. Solomon. New York: Atheneum Books for Young Readers, 2008.

Yolen, Jane. *Not One Damsel in Distress: World Folktales for Strong Girls.* Illustrated by Susan Guevara. San Diego: Silver Whistle Books/ Harcourt, 2000.

CHAPTER 4: POETRY, VERSE, RHYMES, AND SONGS

CITATIONS

Karla Kuskin poem "Thistles" pp. 69–70 from *Dogs & Dragons, Trees & Dreams*, p. 4.

Eloise Greenfield poem "Lessie" pp. 70–71 from *Honey, I Love*, p. [32].

Douglas Florian poem "When Winter" p. 71 from *Handsprings*, p. 8.

Arnold Adoff poem p. 72 from *i am the running girl*, p. [27].

Gwendolyn Brooks poem "Cynthia in the Snow" p. 73 from *Bronzeville Boys and Girl*, p. 12.

Iona and Peter Opie quote p. 75 from *The Oxford Dictionary of Nursery Rhymes*, p. 1.

X. J. Kennedy poem "Lighting a Fire" p. 78 from *The Forgetful Wishing Well*, p. 52.

Paul B. Janeczko quote p. 80 from "Of Poems and Possibilities," p. 8.

Virginia Euwer Wolff quote p. 82 from "An Interview with Virginia Euwer Wolff," by Roger Sutton, p. 282.

SOURCES

Copeland, Jeffrey S. *Speaking of Poets: Interviews with Poets Who Write for Children and Young Adults.* Urbana, IL: National Council of Teachers of English, 1993.

Copeland, Jeffrey S., and Virginia L. Copeland. *Speaking of Poets 2: More Interviews with Poets Who Write for Children and Young Adults.* Urbana, IL: National Council of Teachers of English, 1994.

Deutsch, Babette. *Poetry Handbook: A Dictionary of Terms.* Fourth Edition. New York: Funk & Wagnalls, 1974.

England, Claire, and Adele M. Fasick. *ChildView: Evaluating and Reviewing Materials for Children*. Littleton, CO: Libraries Unlimited, 1987.

Gill, Sharon Ruth. "The Forgotten Genre of Children's Poetry," *The Reading Teacher* 60:7 (April 2007), pp. 622–25.

Hopkins, Lee Bennett. *Pass the Poetry, Please!* Revised, enlarged, and updated 3rd ed. New York: HarperCollins, 1998.

Janeczko, Paul B. "Of Poems and Possibilities," *CSLA Journal* 31:1 (Fall 2007), pp. 8–9.

Korbeck, Sharon. "Children's Poetry: Journeying Beyond the Road Less Traveled," *School Library Journal* 41:4. (April 1995), pp. 43–44.

Leeper, Angela. *Poetry in Literature for Youth: A Guide and Resource Book*. Lanham, MD: Scarecrow, 2006.

Long, Joanna Rudge. "How to Choose a Goose: What Makes a Good Mother Goose," *The Horn Book* 84:1 (January/February 2008), pp. 49–57.

Lukens, Rebecca J. *A Critical Handbook of Children's Literature*. 7th ed. Boston: Allyn and Bacon, 2002.

Opie, Iona, and Peter Opie, eds. *The Oxford Dictionary of Nursery Rhymes*. Oxford: Oxford University Press, 1951.

Sullivan, Ed. "Fiction or Poetry? A Librarian Looks at the Profusion of Novels Written in Verse," *School Library Journal* 49:8 (August 2003), pp. 44–45.

Sutton, Roger. "An Interview with Virginia Euwer Wolff," *The Horn Book* 77:3 (May/June 2001), pp. 280–86.

Whalin, Kathleen. "Becoming Versed in Poetry," *School Library Journal* 42:4 (April 1996), pp. 38–39.

CHILDREN'S BOOKS CITED

Adoff, Arnold. *i am the running girl*. Illustrated by Ronald Himler. New York: Harper & Row, 1979.

Brooks, Gwendolyn. *Bronzeville Boys and Girls*. Illustrated by Faith Ringgold. New York: Amistad/HarperCollins, 2007.

Bryan, Ashley, illus. *Let It Shine: Three Favorite Spirituals*. New York: Atheneum Books for Young Readers, 2007.

Creech, Sharon. *Hate That Cat*. New York: Joanna Cotler Books/HarperCollins, 2008.

———. *Love That Dog*. New York: Joanna Cotler Books/HarperCollins, 2001.

Crews, Nina. *The Neighborhood Mother Goose*. New York: Greenwillow Books, 2004.

Florian, Douglas. *Handsprings: Poems and Paintings*. New York: Greenwillow Books, 2006.

Frost, Helen. *Diamond Willow*. New York: Frances Foster Books/Farrar, Straus, and Giroux, 2008.

———. *Spinning Through the Universe*. New York: Frances Foster Books/Farrar, Straus, and Giroux, 2004.

Gordon, Ruth. *Under All Silences: Shades of Love*. New York: Charlotte Zolotow/Harper & Row, 1987.

Greenfield, Eloise. *Honey, I Love, and Other Love Poems*. Illustrated by Leo and Diane Dillon. New York: Thomas Y. Crowell, 1978.

Hale, Sarah Josepha. *Mary Had a Little Lamb*. Photographs by Bruce McMillan. New York: Scholastic, 1990.

Hinojosa, Tish. *Cada Niño/Every Child: A Bilingual Songbook for Children*. Illustrated by Lucia Angela Perez. El Paso, TX: Cinco Puntos, 2002.

Hopkins, Lee Bennett. *Hamsters, Shells, and Spelling Bees: School Poems*. An I Can Read Book. Illustrated by Sachiko Yoshikawa. New York: HarperCollins, 2008.

———. *Incredible Inventions*. Illustrated by Julia Sarcone-Roach. New York: Greenwillow Books, 2009.

Janeczko, Paul B. *A Foot in the Mouth: Poems to Speak, Sing, and Shout.* Illustrated by Chris Raschka. Somerville, MA: Candlewick, 2009.

Kennedy, X. J. *The Forgetful Wishing Well: Poems for Young People.* Illustrated by Monica Incisa. New York: Margaret K. McElderry/ Atheneum, 1985.

Kuskin, Karla. *Dogs & Dragons, Trees & Dreams: A Collection of Poems.* New York: Harper & Row, 1980.

Langstaff, John M., ed. *Hi! Ho! The Rattlin' Bog, and Other Folk Songs for Group Singing.* New York: Harcourt, Brace & World, 1969.

Larrick, Nancy. *Cats Are Cats.* Illustrated by Ed Young. New York: Philomel Books, 1988.

———. *To the Moon and Back: A Collection of Poems.* Illustrated by Catherine O'Neill. New York: Delacorte, 1991.

Marshall, James, illus. *Old Mother Hubbard and Her Wonderful Dog.* New York: Farrar, Straus, and Giroux, 1991.

Nye, Naomi Shihab. *The Space Between Our Footsteps: Poems and Paintings from the Middle East.* New York: Simon & Schuster, 1998.

———. *What Have You Lost?* Photographs by Michael Nye. New York: Greenwillow Books, 1999.

Opie, Iona, and Peter Opie. *Tail Feathers from Mother Goose: The Opie Rhyme Book.* Boston: Little, Brown, 1988.

Park, Linda Sue. *Tap Dancing on the Roof: Sijo (Poems).* Illustrated by Istvan Banyai. New York: Clarion Books, 2006.

Pearson, Tracey Campbell. *Diddle, Diddle, Dumpling.* New York: Farrar, Straus, and Giroux, 2005.

———. *Little Bo-Peep.* New York: Farrar, Straus, and Giroux, 2004.

———. *Little Miss Muffet.* New York: Farrar, Straus, and Giroux, 2005.

Prelutsky, Jack. *If Not for the Cat: Haiku.* Illustrated by Ted Rand. New York: Greenwillow Books, 2004.

Rosen, Michael J. *The Cuckoo's Haiku*. Illustrated by Stan Fellows. Somerville, MA: Candlewick, 2009.

Ross, Tony. *Three Little Kittens and Other Favorite Nursery Rhymes*. New York: Henry Holt, 2009.

Sanderson, Ruth. *Mother Goose and Friends*. Boston: Little, Brown Young Readers, 2008.

Schnur, Stephen. *Winter: An Alphabet Acrostic*. Illustrated by Leslie Evans. New York: Clarion Books, 2002.

Seeger, Laura Vaccaro. *I Had a Rooster: A Traditional Folk Song*. Foreword by Pete Seeger. New York: Viking, 2001.

Silverstein, Shel. *Falling Up: Poems and Drawings*. New York: HarperCollins, 1996.

———. *A Light in the Attic*. New York: Harper & Row, 1981.

———. *Where the Sidewalk Ends: The Poems and Drawings of Shel Silverstein*. New York: Harper & Row, 1974.

Wolff, Virginia Euwer. *Make Lemonade*. New York: Henry Holt, 1993.

Worth, Valerie. *Small Poems*. Illustrated by Natalie Babbitt. New York: Farrar, Straus, and Giroux, 1972.

Yolen, Jane, and Andrew Fusek Peters. *Here's a Little Poem: A Very First Book of Poetry*. Illustrated by Polly Dunbar. Cambridge, MA: Candlewick, 2007.

CHAPTER 5: PICTURE BOOKS

CITATIONS

Dilys Evans quote p. 87 from "An Extraordinary Vision: Picture Books of the Nineties," p. 759.

Margaret Wise Brown quote p. 89 from *The Indoor Noisy Book*, p. [16].

Margaret Wise Brown quotes pp. 92–93 from *The Runaway Bunny*, pp. [8–9] and [12–13].

Margaret Wise Brown quote p. 94 from *The Little Island*, pp. [9], [11], [13], [15], and [17].

Timothy M. Rivinus and Lisa Audet quote p. 102 from "The Psychological Genius of Margaret Wise Brown," p. 10.

Lane Smith quote p. 109 from "How I Learned to Love the Computer," p. 53.

SOURCES

Association for Library Service to Children. *The Newbery and Caldecott Awards: A Guide to the Medal and Honor Books*, 2009 ed. Chicago: American Library Association, 2009.

Bader, Barbara. *American Picturebooks from Noah's Ark to The Beast Within*. New York: Macmillan, 1976.

Bang, Molly. *Picture This: How Pictures Work*. New York: SeaStar Books, 2000.

Behrmann, Christine. "The Media Used in Caldecott Medal Picture Books: Notes Toward a Definitive List," *Journal of Youth Services in Libraries* 1:2 (Winter 1988), pp. 198–212.

Cianciolo, Patricia J. *Picture Books for Children*. 4th ed. Chicago: American Library Association, 1997.

Couch, Tony. *Tony Couch's Keys to Successful Painting*. Cincinnati, OH: North Light Books, 1992.

Evans, Dilys. "An Extraordinary Vision," *The Horn Book* 67:6 (November/December 1991), pp. 712–15.

———. "An Extraordinary Vision: Picture Books of the Nineties," *The Horn Book* 66:6 (November/December, 1992), pp. 759–63.

———. *Show and Tell: Exploring the Fine Art of Children's Book Illustration*. San Francisco: Chronicle Books, 2008.

Griffith, Thomas. *A Practical Guide for Beginning Painters*. Englewood Cliffs, NJ: Prentice Hall, 1981.

Hands, Nancy S. *Illustrating Children's Books: A Guide to Drawing, Printing, and Publishing.* New York: Prentice Hall, 1986.

Henkes, Kevin. "Illustration in Children's Books: Printmaking Techniques." Selected bibliography compiled, printed, and distributed by the Cooperative Children's Book Center, Madison, WI, May 1982.

Karl, Jean E. *How to Write and Sell Children's Picture Books.* Cincinnati, OH: Writer's Digest Books, 1994.

Kiefer, Barbara. "Visual Criticism and Children's Literature," in *Evaluating Children's Books: A Critical Look.* Edited by Betsy Hearne and Roger Sutton. Urbana-Champaign, IL: University of Illinois, 1993, pp. 73–91.

Lacy, Lyn Ellen. *Art and Design in Children's Picture Books: An Analysis of Caldecott Award-Winning Illustrations.* Chicago: American Library Association, 1986.

Lane, Heather. "Don't Judge Art by Its Medium: Should Computer-Generated Illustrations Be Caldecott-Worthy?" *Children and Libraries* 4:1 (Spring 2006), pp. 28–29.

Lodge, Sally. "Don and Audrey Wood Go Digital," *Publishers Weekly* 243 (September 2, 1996), p. 40.

Lurie, Stephanie. "First the Word: An Editor's View of Picture Book Texts," *School Library Journal* 37:10 (October 1991), pp. 50–51.

MacCann, Donnarae, and Olga Richard. *The Child's First Books: A Critical Study of Pictures and Texts.* New York: H. W. Wilson, 1973.

Marantz, Kenneth A., and Sylvia S. Marantz. *Creating Picture Books: Interviews with Editors, Art Directors, Reviewers, Booksellers, Professors, Librarians and Showcasers.* Jefferson, N.C.: McFarland, 1997.

Marcus, Leonard S. *Margaret Wise Brown: Awakened by the Moon.* Boston, MA: Beacon, 1992.

———. "Medal Man: Randolph Caldecott and the Art of the Picture Book," *The Horn Book* 77:2 (March/April 2001), pp. 155–70.

Nikolajeva, Maria, and Carole Scott. *How Picturebooks Work*. New York: Garland, 2000.

Osterweil, Wendy. "Drawing in Children's Book Illustration." Selected bibliography compiled, printed, and distributed by the Cooperative Children's Book Center, Madison, WI, May 1985.

———. "Painting Media in Children's Book Illustration." Selected bibliography compiled, printed, and distributed by the Cooperative Children's Book Center, Madison, WI, June 1984.

Rivinus, Timothy, and Lisa Audet. "The Psychological Genius of Margaret Wise Brown," *Children's Literature in Education* 23:1 (June 1992), pp. 1–14.

Saylor, David. "Look Again: An Art Director Offers Some Pointers on 'Learning to See,'" *School Library Journal* 46:1 (January 2000), pp. 37–38.

Shulevitz, Uri. *Writing with Pictures: How to Write and Illustrate Children's Books*. New York: Watson-Guptill, 1985.

Smith, Lane. "How I Learned to Love the Computer," *School Library Journal* 48:11 (November 2002), pp. 52–55.

Stewig, John Warren. *Looking at Picture Books*. Fort Atkinson, WI: Highsmith, 1995.

Zelinsky, Paul O. "Artist's Notes on the Creation of *Rapunzel*," *Journal of Youth Services in Libraries* 11:3 (Spring 1998), pp. 214–17.

CHILDREN'S BOOKS CITED

Andersen, Hans Christian. *The Ugly Duckling*. Adapted and illustrated by Jerry Pinkney. New York: William Morrow, 1999.

Bang, Molly. *Ten Nine Eight*. New York: Greenwillow Books, 1983.

Brown, Margaret Wise. *Another Important Book*. Illustrated by Chris Raschka. New York: Joanna Cotler/HarperCollins, 1999.

————. *Goodnight Moon.* Illustrated by Clement Hurd. New York: Harper & Row, 1947.

————. *The Indoor Noisy Book.* Illustrated by Leonard Weisgard. New York: W. R. Scott, 1942.

————. [Golden MacDonald, pseud.]. *The Little Island.* Illustrated by Leonard Weisgard. New York: Doubleday, 1946.

————. *The Runaway Bunny.* Illustrated by Clement Hurd. New York: Harper & Row, 1942.

Burton, Virginia Lee. *The Little House.* Boston: Houghton Mifflin, 1942.

Campbell, Nicola I. *Shin-chi's Canoe.* Illustrated by Kim LaFave. Toronto: Groundwood Books, 2008.

Coy, John. *Night Driving.* Illustrated by Peter McCarty. New York: Henry Holt, 1996.

Crews, Nina. *Below.* New York: Henry Holt, 2006.

————. *The Neighborhood Mother Goose.* New York: Greenwillow Books, 2004.

Cronin, Doreen. *Diary of a Worm.* Illustrated by Harry Bliss. New York: Joanna Cotler Books/HarperCollins, 2003.

Ehlert, Lois. *Leaf Man.* San Diego: Harcourt, 2005.

Fisher, Aileen. *The Story Goes On.* Illustrated by Mique Moriuchi. Brookfield, CT: Roaring Brook, 2005.

Frame, Jeron Ashford. *Yesterday I Had the Blues.* Illustrated by R. Gregory Christie. Berkeley, CA: Tricycle, 2003.

Frazee, Marla. *A Couple of Boys Have the Best Week Ever.* San Diego: Harcourt, 2008.

Gág, Wanda. *Millions of Cats.* New York: Coward-McCann, 1928.

Geisert, Arthur. *Lights Out.* Boston: Walter Lorraine/Houghton Mifflin, 2005.

———. *Nursery Crimes*. Boston: Walter Lorraine/Houghton Mifflin, 2001.

Goble, Paul. *Iktomi and the Buzzard: A Plains Indian Story*. New York: Orchard Books, 1994.

Graham, Bob. *How to Heal a Broken Wing*. Cambridge, MA: Candlewick, 2008.

Grey, Mini. *Traction Man Is Here!* New York: Alfred A. Knopf, 2005.

Hall, Donald. *Ox-Cart Man*. Illustrated by Barbara Cooney. New York: Viking, 1979.

Hoban, Tana. *So Many Circles, So Many Squares*. New York: Greenwillow Books, 1998.

Hole, Stian. *Garmann's Summer*. Translated from the Norwegian by Dan Bartlett. Grand Rapids, MI: Eerdmans Books for Young Readers, 2008.

Jenkins, Steve. *Actual Size*. Boston: Houghton Mifflin, 2004.

Jenkins, Steve, and Robin Page. *What Do You Do with a Tail Like This?* Boston: Houghton Mifflin, 2003.

Johnson, Angela. *Just Like Josh Gibson*. Illustrated by Beth Peck. New York: Simon & Schuster, 2004.

Johnson-Davies, Denys. *Goha, the Wise Fool*. Illustrated by Hag Hamdy and Hany. Sewing by Hany El Saed Ahmed from drawings by Hag Hamdy Mohamed Fattouh. New York: Philomel, 2005.

Levine, Ellen. *I Hate English!* Illustrated by Steve Björkman. New York: Scholastic, 1989.

Look, Lenore. *Henry's First-Moon Birthday*. Illustrated by Yumi Heo. New York: Anne Schwartz/Atheneum Books for Young Readers, 2001.

Low, William. *Machines Go to Work*. New York: Henry Holt, 2009.

Martin, Jacqueline Briggs. *Snowflake Bentley*. Illustrated by Mary

Azarian. Boston: Houghton Mifflin, 1998.

McCarty, Peter. *Moon Plane*. New York: Henry Holt, 2006.

McMillan, Bruce. *Fire Engine Shapes*. New York: Lothrop, Lee & Shepard, 1988.

Miller, Margaret. *Guess Who?* New York: Greenwillow Books, 1994.

Morales, Yuyi. *Just a Minute: A Trickster Tale and Counting Book*. San Francisco: Chronicle Books, 2003.

Myers, Christopher. *Wings*. New York: Scholastic, 2000.

Njeng, Pierre Ives. *Vacation in the Village: A Story from West Africa*. Honesdale, PA: Boyds Mills, 1999.

Raschka, Chris. *Mysterious Thelonious*. New York: Orchard Books, 1997.

Seeger, Laura Vaccaro. *First the Egg*. New Milford, CT: Neal Porter/Roaring Brook, 2007.

Sidman, Joyce. *Song of the Water Boatman, and Other Pond Poems*. Illustrated by Beckie Prange. Boston: Houghton Mifflin, 2005.

Smith, Charles R. *Loki & Alex: The Adventures of a Dog and His Best Friend*. New York: Dutton Children's Books, 2001.

Steptoe, Javaka. *In Daddy's Arms I Am Tall: African Americans Celebrating Fathers*. New York: Lee & Low, 1997.

Steptoe, John. *Mufaro's Beautiful Daughters: An African Tale*. New York: Lothrop, Lee & Shepard, 1987.

———. *Stevie*. New York: Harper & Row, 1969.

Swanson, Susan Marie. *The House in the Night*. Illustrated by Beth Krommes. Boston: Houghton Mifflin, 2008.

Wiesner, David. *Flotsam*. New York: Clarion Books, 2006.

Willems, Mo. *Don't Let the Pigeon Drive the Bus!* New York: Hyperion, 2003.

Williams, Vera B. *A Chair for My Mother*. New York: Greenwillow Books, 1982.

Winter, Jonah. *Frida*. Illustrated by Ana Juan. Arthur A. Levine Books/Scholastic, 2002.

Xiong, Blia. *Nine-in-One, Grr! Grr! A Folktale from the Hmong People of Laos*. Adapted by Cathy Spagnoli. Illustrated by Nancy Hom. San Francisco, CA: Children's Book Press, 1989.

Yolen, Jane. *The Emperor and the Kite*. Illustrated by Ed Young. Cleveland: World, 1967.

Young, Ed. *High on a Hill: A Book of Chinese Riddles*. New York: Collins, 1980.

———. *Lon Po Po: A Red-Riding Hood Story from China*. New York: Philomel Books, 1989.

———. *Seven Blind Mice*. New York: Philomel Books, 1982.

Zelinsky, Paul O. *Rapunzel*. New York: Dutton Children's Books, 1997.

Zolotow, Charlotte. *Mr. Rabbit and the Lovely Present*. Illustrated by Maurice Sendak. New York: Harper & Row, 1962.

CHAPTER 6: EASY READERS AND TRANSITIONAL BOOKS

CITATIONS

John Hersey quote pp. 114–15 from "Why Do Students Bog Down with the First R?: A Local Committee Sheds Light on a National Problem: Reading," p. 148.

Arnold Lobel quote pp. 116–17 from *Frog and Toad Are Friends*, pp. 20–24.

Dr. Seuss quote pp. 121–22 from *The Cat in the Hat*, p. 25.

Dori Chaconas quote p. 122 from *Cork & Fuzz*, p. 19.

Else Holmelund Minarik quote p. 122 from *Little Bear*, p. 24.

Ruth Horowitz quote pp. 123–24 from *Breakout at the Bug Lab*, pp. 5–6.

Mo Willems quote p. 129 from *There Is a Bird on Your Head*, pp. 12–22.

David Milgrim quote pp. 129–30 from *See Pip Point*, p. [15].

Erica Silverman quote pp. 130–31 from *Cowgirl Kate and Cocoa*, pp. [25–27].

Kate DiCamillo quote pp. 131–32 from *Mercy Watson Goes for a Ride*, pp. 36–37.

Ann Cameron quote p. 133 from *The Stories Julian Tells*, p. 37.

Lenore Look quote p. 134 from *Ruby Lu, Brave and True*, pp. 6–7.

Anne Fine quote from p. 134 *The Jamie and Angus Stories*, pp. 102–103.

Celia Barker Lottridge quotes p. 136 from *Berta: A Remarkable Dog*, pp. 11, 15, 25, 31, 40.

Sources

Adams, Marilyn Jager. *Beginning to Read: Thinking and Learning About Print*. Cambridge, MA: MIT Press, 1990.

Asselin, Marlene. "Texts for Beginning Readers: The Critical Match Between Reader and Text," *Teacher Librarian* 28:2 (December 2000), pp. 58–59.

Barstow, Barbara, Judith Riggle, and Leslie Molnar. *Beyond Picture Books: Subject Access to Best Books for Beginning Readers*. 3rd ed. Westport, CT: Libraries Unlimited, 2008.

Bean, Joy. "In Search of New Readers," *Publishers Weekly* 251 (May 31, 2004), pp. 30–31.

Hersey, John. "Why Do Students Bog Down with the First R?: A Local Committee Sheds Light on a National Problem: Reading," *Life* 36:21 (May 24, 1954), pp. 136–50.

Jacobson, Jennifer Richard. "Helping Students Make the Leap from Beginning Readers to Chapter Books," *Knowledge Quest* 32:1 (September/October 2003), pp. 37–38.

Jensen, Margaret. "Books for Beginning Readers: A Bibliography of Trade Books for Young Children." Selected bibliography compiled, printed, and distributed by the Cooperative Children's Book Center. Madison, WI, April 1984.

———. "Characteristics of Trade Books." Books for Beginning Readers Workshop, May 3, 1984 (audiotape). Madison, WI: Cooperative Children's Book Center, University of Wisconsin–Madison, 1984.

Jensen, Margaret, Kathleen T. Horning, Ginny Moore Kruse, and Deana Grobe. "Young Fiction: Books for Transitional Readers." Selected bibliography compiled, printed, and distributed by the Cooperative Children's Book Center. Madison, WI, April 1989.

Kruse, Ginny Moore. "Read-Alouds? Think Again: The True Purpose of the Geisel Children's Book Award," *School Library Journal* 53:6 (June 2007), pp. 36–37.

Lambert, Megan. "Informed Reading: Evaluating and Using Picture Books, Beginning Reader Books, and Illustrated Books," *Children and Libraries* 4:3 (Winter 2006), pp. 31–34, 54.

MacDonald, Ruth K. *Dr. Seuss*. Boston: Twayne, 1988.

Maughan, Shannon. "Readers for Early Readers," *Publishers Weekly* 247 (May 22, 2000), pp. 40–43.

Mogilner, Alijandra. *Children's Writer's Word Book*. Cincinnati, OH: Writer's Digest Books, 1992.

Stanley, Sarah, and Brian W. Sturm. "Sequential Art Books and Beginning Readers: Can the Pictures Help Them Decode Words?" *Knowledge Quest* 37:2 (November/December, 2008), pp. 50–57.

Ward, Caroline. "Best of Beginning Readers: Theodor Seuss Geisel Award Launched by ALSC," *Children and Libraries* 3:2 (Summer/Fall, 2005), pp. 41, 61.

CHILDREN'S BOOKS CITED

Bauer, Marion Dane. *The Blue Ghost*. A Stepping Stone Book. Illustrated by Suling Wang. New York: Random House, 2005.

Cameron, Ann. *Julian's Glorious Summer*. A Stepping Stone Book. Illustrated by Dora Leder. New York: Random House, 1987.

———. *More Stories Julian Tells*. Illustrated by Ann Strugnell. New York: Random House, 1989.

———. *The Stories Julian Tells*. Illustrated by Ann Strugnell. New York: Pantheon Books, 1981.

Chaconas, Dori. *Cork & Fuzz*. Viking Easy-to-Read. Illustrated by Lisa McCue. New York: Viking, 2005.

DiCamillo, Kate. *Mercy Watson Goes for a Ride*. Illustrated by Chris Van Dusen. Cambridge, MA: Candlewick, 2006.

Edwards, Michelle. *Pa Lia's First Day*. Jackson Friends, Book 1. San Diego: Harcourt, Brace, 1999.

Fine, Anne. *The Jamie and Angus Stories*. Illustrated by Penny Dale. Cambridge, MA: Candlewick, 2002.

Haas, Jessie. *Runaway Radish*. Illustrated by Margot Apple. New York: Greenwillow Books, 2001.

Horowitz, Ruth. *Breakout at the Bug Lab*. Dial Easy-to-Read. Illustrated by Joan Holub. New York: Dial Books for Young Readers, 2001.

Lobel, Arnold. *Frog and Toad Are Friends*. An I Can Read Book. New York: Harper & Row, 1970.

Look, Lenore. *Ruby Lu, Brave and True*. Illustrated by Anne Wilsdorf. New York: Anne Schwartz/Atheneum, 2004.

Lottridge, Celia Barker. *Berta: A Remarkable Dog*. Illustrated by Elsa Myotte. Toronto: Groundwood Books, 2002.

Milgrim, David. *See Pip Point*. Ready-to-Read. New York: Atheneum Books for Young Readers, 2003.

Minarik, Else Holmelund. *Little Bear*. An I Can Read Book. Illustrated by Maurice Sendak. New York: Harper & Row, 1957.

Rylant, Cynthia. *Henry and Mudge: The First Book*. Ready-to-Read. Illustrated by Suçie Stevenson. New York: Bradbury, 1987.

Seuss, Dr. *The Cat in the Hat*. Beginner Books. New York: Random House, 1957.

Silverman, Erica. *Cowgirl Kate and Cocoa*. Illustrated by Betsy Lewin. San Diego: Harcourt, 2005.

Willems, Mo. *There Is a Bird on Your Head*. An Elephant & Piggie Book. New York: Hyperion, 2007.

CHAPTER 7: FICTION

CITATIONS

Anne Carroll Moore quote p. 139 from *My Roads to Childhood*, p. 23.

Louise P. Latimer quote p. 140 from "They Who Get Slapped," p. 626.

Jacqueline Woodson quotes pp. 153–54, 154–55, 155 from *After Tupac and D Foster*, pp. 24, 14, 62–63.

Kevin Henkes quotes pp. 159, 160, 161 from *Words of Stone*, pp. 17, 77, 52, 7, 1, 113, 151, 85, 84, 40, 116, 23, 41, 40.

Christopher Paul Curtis quote p. 162 from *Bud, Not Buddy*, pp. 93–94.

Christopher Paul Curtis quote p. 162 from *Elijah of Buxton*, p. 80.

SOURCES

Baker, Deidre F. "Poetry in Prose," *The Horn Book* 81:3 (May/June 2005), pp. 271–79.

Corbett, Sue. "Reality Check for Fantasy," *Publishers Weekly* 253 (July 17, 2006), pp. 57–59.

England, Claire, and Adele M. Fasick. *ChildView: Evaluating and Reviewing Materials for Children*. Littleton, CO: Libraries Unlimited, 1987.

Johnson, Deidre. *Stratemeyer Pseudonyms and Series Books: An Annotated Checklist of Stratemeyer and Stratemeyer Syndicate Publications*. Westport, CT: Greenwood, 1982.

Latimer, Louise P. "They Who Get Slapped," *Library Journal* 49 (July 1924), pp. 623–26.

Lukens, Rebecca J. *A Critical Handbook of Children's Literature.* 7th ed. Boston: Allyn and Bacon, 2002.

Mendlesohn, Farah. "The Campaign for Shiny Futures," *The Horn Book* 85:2 (March/April 2009), pp. 155–61.

Moore, Anne Carroll. *My Roads to Childhood: Views and Reviews of Children's Books.* New York: Doubleday, Doran, 1939.

Peters, John. "Scary Fun: Stories to Scare Your Socks Off," *School Library Journal* 53:10 (October 2007), pp. 56–61.

Vandergrift, Kay E. *Child and Story: The Literary Connection.* New York: Neal-Schuman, 1980.

Volz, Bridget Dealy, Cheryl Perkins Scheer, and Lynda Blackburn Welborn. *Junior Genreflecting: A Guide to Good Reads and Series Fiction for Children.* Englewood, CO: Libraries Unlimited, 2000.

Wadham, Tim. "Plot Does Matter," *The Horn Book* 75:4 (July/August 1999), pp. 445–50.

CHILDREN'S BOOKS CITED

Appelt, Kathi. *The Underneath.* Illustrated by David Small. New York: Atheneum Books for Young Readers, 2008.

Avi. *Nothing But the Truth: A Documentary Novel.* New York: Orchard Books, 1991.

Broach, Elise. *Masterpiece.* Illustrated by Kelly Murphy. New York: Henry Holt, 2008.

Cleary, Beverly. *Ramona the Pest.* Illustrated by Louis Darling. New York: William Morrow, 1968.

Clements, Andrew. *No Talking.* Illustrated by Mark Elliott. New York: Simon & Schuster, 2007.

Collins, Suzanne. *The Hunger Games.* New York: Scholastic, 2008.

Creech, Sharon. *Walk Two Moons.* New York: HarperCollins, 1994.

Curtis, Christopher Paul. *Bud, Not Buddy*. New York: Delacorte, 1999.

———. *Elijah of Buxton*. New York: Scholastic, 2007.

Cushman, Karen. *The Loud Silence of Francine Green*. New York: Clarion Books, 2006.

———. *The Midwife's Apprentice*. New York: Clarion Books, 1995.

DiCamillo, Kate. *The Miraculous Journey of Edward Tulane*. Illustrated by Bagram Ibatoulline. Cambridge, MA: Candlewick, 2006.

Erdrich, Louise. *The Birchbark House*. Illustrated by the author. New York: Hyperion, 1999.

Farmer, Nancy. *The House of the Scorpion*. New York: Richard Jackson/Atheneum Books for Young Readers, 2002.

Fleischman, Paul. *Bull Run*. Illustrated by David Frampton. New York: Laura Geringer/HarperCollins, 1993.

Fleming, Candace. *The Fabled Fourth Graders of Aesop Elementary School*. New York: Schwartz & Wade/Random House, 2007.

Frost, Helen. *Diamond Willow*. New York: Farrar, Straus, and Giroux, 2008.

Gaiman, Neil. *Coraline*. Illustrated by Dave McKean. New York: HarperCollins, 2002.

Hale, Shannon. *Princess Academy*. New York: Bloomsbury Children's Books, 2005.

Hamilton, Virginia. *The Magical Adventures of Pretty Pearl*. New York: Charlotte Zolotow/Harper & Row, 1983.

Hawes, Charles Boardman. *The Dark Frigate*. Boston: Atlantic Monthly, 1924.

Henkes, Kevin. *Bird Lake Moon*. New York: Greenwillow Books, 2008.

———. *Words of Stone*. New York: Greenwillow Books, 1992.

Holm, Jennifer L. *Babymouse: Queen of the World*. Illustrated by Matthew Holm. New York: Random House, 2005.

Law, Ingrid. *Savvy*. New York: Dial Books for Young Readers, 2008.

Lowry, Lois. *The Giver*. Boston: Houghton Mifflin, 1993.

———. *Number the Stars*. Boston: Houghton Mifflin, 1989.

O'Connor, Barbara. *How to Steal a Dog*. New York: Frances Foster/ Farrar, Straus, and Giroux, 2007.

Orlev, Uri. *Run, Boy, Run: A Novel*. Translated from the Hebrew by Hillel Halkin. Boston: Walter Lorraine/Houghton Mifflin, 2003.

Paulsen, Gary. *Hatchet*. New York: Bradbury, 1987.

Philbrick, Rodman. *The Young Man and the Sea*. New York: Blue Sky/ Scholastic, 2004.

Preller, James. *Six Innings: A Game in the Life*. New York: Feiwel & Friends, 2008.

Sachar, Louis. *Holes*. New York: Frances Foster/Farrar, Straus, and Giroux, 1998.

Selznick, Brian. *The Invention of Hugo Cabret: A Novel in Words and Pictures*. New York: Scholastic, 2007.

Soo, Kean. *Jellaby*. New York: Hyperion, 2008.

Spinelli, Jerry. *Wringer*. New York: Joanna Cotler/HarperCollins, 1997.

Stead, Rebecca. *When You Reach Me*. New York: Wendy Lamb Books/ Random House, 2009.

Taylor, Mildred D. *Roll of Thunder, Hear My Cry*. New York: Dial, 1976.

Woodson, Jacqueline. *After Tupac and D Foster*. New York: Putnam, 2008.

CHAPTER 8: WRITING A REVIEW

CITATIONS

Virginia Woolf quote p. 165 from "Reviewing," in *The Captain's Death Bed and Other Essays*, p. 130.

Paul Heins quotes pp. 167, 167–68 from "Out on a Limb with the Critics: Some Random Thoughts on the Present State of the Criticism of Children's Literature," pp. 269, 268.

Phyllis K. Kennemer quote pp. 173–74 from "Reviews of Fiction Books:

How They Differ," p. 419.

Betsy Hearne quote p. 175 from "A Reviewer's Story," p. 82.

Zena Sutherland quote p. 175 from "A Life in Review," p. 360.

Kathleen T. Horning quote p. 176 from Review of *Shortcut* by David Macaulay, p. 4.

Deborah Stevenson quote pp. 176–77 from Review of *Me Hungry!* by Jeremy Tankard, p. 356.

Roger Sutton quote p. 177 from Review of *Carl's Summer Vacation* by Alexandra Day, pp. 432–33.

Ilene Cooper quote pp. 177–78 from Review of *Chicken Little* by Rebecca and Ed Emberley, p. 80.

John Rowe Townsend quote p. 180 from "The Reviewing of Children's Books," in *Celebrating Children's Books*, p. 187.

Sources

Bird, Elizabeth. "Blogging in the Kidlitosphere," *The Horn Book* 83:3 (May/June 2007), pp. 305–309.

Burns, Elizabeth. "Curl Up with a Cup of Tea and a Good Blog," *School Library Journal* 53:2 (February 2007), pp. 40–42.

Cooper, Ilene. Review of *Chicken Little* by Rebecca and Ed Emberley, *Booklist* 105:17 (May 1, 2009), p. 80.

Craver, Kathleen W. "Book Reviewers: An Empirical Portrait," *School Library Media Quarterly* 12:5 (Fall 1984), pp. 383–409.

Darling, Richard L. *The Rise of Children's Book Reviewing in America, 1865–1881*. New York: Bowker, 1968.

Drewry, John E. *Writing Book Reviews*. Boston: The Writer, 1966.

Elleman, Barbara. "A Sentimental Journey," *Booklist* 81:21 (July 1985), p. 1551.

Hearne, Betsy. "A Reviewer's Story," *Library Quarterly* 51:1 (January 1981), pp. 80–87.

————. "What's New?" *The Horn Book* 82:5 (September/October 2006), pp. 541–45.

Heins, Paul. "Out on a Limb with the Critics: Some Random Thoughts on the Present State of the Criticism of Children's Literature," *The Horn Book* 46:3 (June 1970), pp. 264–73.

Heppermann, Christine. "Looking like a Wonton and Talking like a Fortune Cookie," *The Horn Book* 78:2 (March/April 2002), pp. 153–57.

Horning, Kathleen T. Review of *Shortcut* by David Macaulay, Milwaukee *Journal Sentinel*, November 14, 1995, p. 4.

Kammerman, Sylvia E., ed. *Book Reviewing: A Guide to Writing Reviews for Newspapers, Magazines, Radio, and Television.* Boston: The Writer, 1978.

Kennemer, Phyllis K. "Reviews of Fiction Books: How They Differ," *Top of the News* 40:4 (Summer 1984), pp. 419–22.

Kirch, Claire. "Jessa Crispin Rewrites the Rules of Reviewing," *Publishers Weekly* 255 (January 14, 2008), p. 21.

McCanse, Ralph Alan. *The Art of the Book Review: A Comprehensive Working Outline.* Madison, WI: University of Wisconsin Press, 1963.

Silver, Linda R. "Criticism, Reviewing and the Library Review Media," *Top of the News* 35:2 (Winter 1979), pp. 123–30.

Stevenson, Deborah. "Finding Literary Goodness in a Pluralistic World," *The Horn Book* 82:5 (September/October 2006), pp. 511–17.

————. Review of *Me Hungry!* by Jeremy Tankard, *The Bulletin of the Center for Children's Books* 61:8 (April 2008), p. 356.

Sutherland, Zena. "A Life in Review," *Journal of Youth Services in Libraries* 9:4 (Summer 1996), pp. 357–65.

Sutton, Roger. Review of *Carl's Summer Vacation* by Alexandra Day, *The Horn Book* 84:4 (July/August 2008), pp. 432–33.

Thomson, Ashley. "How to Review a Book," *Canadian Library Journal* 48:6 (December 1991), pp. 416–18.

Townsend, John Rowe. "The Reviewing of Children's Books," in *Celebrating Children's Books: Essays on Children's Literature in Honor of Zena Sutherland*. Edited by Betsy Hearne and Marilyn Kaye. New York: Lothrop, Lee & Shepard Books, 1981, pp. 165–87.

Walford, A. J., ed. *Reviews and Reviewing: A Guide*. Phoenix, AZ: Oryx, 1986.

"What Makes a Good Review?: Ten Experts Speak," *Top of the News* 35:2 (Winter 1979), pp. 146–52.

Woolf, Virginia. "Reviewing," in *The Captain's Death Bed and Other Essays*. New York: Harcourt, Brace, 1950, pp. 127–42.

CHILDREN'S BOOKS CITED

Day, Alexandra. *Carl's Summer Vacation*. New York: Farrar, Straus, and Giroux, 2008.

Delano, Marfé Ferguson. *Helen's Eyes: A Photobiography of Annie Sullivan, Helen Keller's Teacher*. Washington, D.C.: National Geographic, 2008.

Dowd, Siobhan. *The London Eye Mystery*. New York: David Fickling Books/Random House, 2008.

Emberley, Rebecca, and Ed Emberley. *Chicken Little*. New York: Neal Porter/Roaring Brook, 2009.

Gaiman, Neil. *The Graveyard Book*. Illustrated by Dave McKean. New York: HarperCollins, 2008.

Macaulay, David. *Black and White*. Boston: Houghton Mifflin, 1990.

———. *Shortcut*. Boston: Houghton Mifflin, 1995.

———. *The Way Things Work*. Boston: Houghton Mifflin, 1988.

Tankard, Jeremy. *Me Hungry!* Cambridge, MA: Candlewick, 2008.

in picture books, 90

rhythm, 68, 70–71

  in fictional style, 161

  in picture books, 89–90

Riordan, Rick, 143

Rise of Children's Book Reviewing in America, 1865–1881, The (Darling), 165

Rivinus, Dr. Timothy M., 102

Robert F. Sibert Informational Book Medal, 27

Rocky and Bullwinkle, 66

Rosen, Michael J., 79, 81

Ross, Tony, 75

roughs, 9

Rowling, J. K., 143

Ruby Lu, Brave and True (Look), 134

Run, Boy, Run (Orlev), 142

Runaway Bunny, The (M. W. Brown), 92–93

Runaway Radish (Haas), 135

Rylant, Cynthia, 125–26

Sachar, Louis, 147, 150–51

Sanderson, Ruth, 75–76

Santoro, Christopher, 29

Sattler, Helen Roney, 29

Savvy (Law), 142–43

Scary Stories to Tell in the Dark (Schwartz), 64–65

Schnur, Stephen, 79

School Library Journal, 10, 166

school stories, 141

Schwartz, Alvin, 64–65

science books, photography in, 35–36

science fiction, 143

Scientists in the Field series, 36

Scieszka, Jon, 66

scrapbook style, 37–38

secondary sources, 45

Secrets of a Civil War Submarine (Walker), 41–42

See Pip Point (Milgram), 129–30

Seeger, Laura Vaccaro, 84, 106

Seeger, Pete, 84

Selznick, Brian, 144

Sendak, Maurice, 87, 111

sentences

  length of in easy readers, 122–23

  in transitional books, 133–34

series books, 139. *See also specific series names*

setting, in fiction, 157–58

Seuss, Dr. (Theodor Seuss Geisel), 115, 117–18, 121–22, 123

Seven Blind Mice (Young), 112

shape (in art), 96–97

Shinchi's Canoe (Campbell), 109

Shortcut (Macaulay), 176

Sibert Medal, 34

Sidman, Joyce, 107

sight words, 119

sijo, 80

Silverman, Erica, 130–31